MW00936516

The Gift

A Spiritual adventure

A Young Boy's Dream,
A Young Man's Goal,
An Old Man's Discovery

David Ward Sandidge

WESTBOW
PRESS
A DIVISION OF THOMAS NELSON
& ZONDERVAN

Copyright © 2015 David Ward Sandidge.

All rights reserved. No part of this book may be used or reproduced by
any means, graphic, electronic, or mechanical, including photocopying,
recording, taping or by any information storage retrieval system
without the written permission of the publisher except in the case
of brief quotations embodied in critical articles and reviews.

Scripture quotations taken from the Holy Bible, New Living Translation,
Copyright © 1996, 2004. Used by permission of Tyndale House
Publishers, Inc., Wheaton, Illinois 60189. All rights reserved.

Quotes from the Bible are taken from the Life Application Bible,
New Living Translation, Tyndale House Publishers, Inc. 1996

WestBow Press books may be ordered through
booksellers or by contacting:

WestBow Press
A Division of Thomas Nelson & Zondervan
1663 Liberty Drive
Bloomington, IN 47403
www.westbowpress.com
1 (866) 928-1240

Because of the dynamic nature of the Internet, any web addresses or
links contained in this book may have changed since publication and
may no longer be valid. The views expressed in this work are solely those
of the author and do not necessarily reflect the views of the publisher,
and the publisher hereby disclaims any responsibility for them.

Any people depicted in stock imagery provided by Thinkstock are
models, and such images are being used for illustrative purposes only.
Certain stock imagery © Thinkstock.

ISBN: 978-1-4908-5125-9 (sc)

Library of Congress Control Number: 2015902644

Print information available on the last page.

WestBow Press rev. date: 03/13/2015

Contents

For Ethan, Jack, Tracy, and Balian. Remember, the gift is free for the asking.

Foreword

I was encouraged to write a short foreword so that you could get an idea of what I was trying to write about before becoming totally frustrated and quitting before reaching the good part, wherever that is. I never liked forewords. In the past I always thought they got in the way of the action in the story. But I always skimmed through them anyway because, hidden within their inceptive pages there might have been something important, something tangible that brought everything together at the end of the story. Well, there's not much action in this book. But there are some wonderful moments from the collective histories of a few colorful people forever documented between its covers.

Did you ever feel like you wished you had had a movie camera back whenever so you could have filmed the events and the people you never thought you'd lose? Was there ever a time in your life when you thought you were truly contented, really happy? It's commonly thought that we can't go back, but if you could close your eyes and return to that place at that time for just a brief few moments would you feel the same about it as you felt back then?

This book is about pictures; pictures in your mind; pictures of yourself in the story; pictures of your past and your present, and perhaps, your future. The conclusion of the story is open-ended; therefore, you must derive your own epilogue. You must come to a decision, and I believe it is the most important decision you will ever make in your entire life.

Chapter One

The Gift is Given

One hot summer afternoon many years ago when I was but fifteen years old, Mr. Hillman paused briefly during our short walk to the little training airplane we were about to take aloft. He said he had something to give me. I couldn't imagine what it was. He reached into his pocket to retrieve a small gray jewelry box; it looked brand new. Before giving it to me he said these words:

"David, I want to give you this gift because I know that someday you're going to fly for a major airline. I can't recommend it because I expect that it may one day destroy the passion you have in your heart for aviation. But I know you're going to make flying your profession. So I want you to have this.

"There are two items in this box; one is more important in what it represents than the other one is, but they are linked inexorably together for a reason. Not simply to form the gift in the box, but for a much deeper meaning than that. There is a duality in their purpose together. Each of the two elements of this gift represents something very important that you will need to find in your own life.

"I want you to take this gift and keep it until you discover the meaning behind each element and what they represent together. It may take years for you to discover these things, or it could happen tomorrow. But I want you to promise me that after you do find it you will someday pass this gift on to another youngster. You'll know when that time comes, and you'll know who that young person is. Do you promise me that you'll do this?"

I was puzzled, and I didn't know what else to say except, "Yes, I promise."

He handed me the box, put an arm around my shoulder and then said, "Now, let's go shoot some landings."

Chapter Two

Passing the Torch, Part One

A sudden rush of euphoria came over me swiftly out of nowhere it seemed as I sipped my coffee from the Styrofoam cup in my hand. All was right with the world. I was at the right place, at the right time, and with the right qualifications….

"Here I am, literally at the top of the world, sitting in my command position watching over a multi-million dollar piece of equipment as it propels itself swiftly through the rarified air at thirty-nine thousand feet above the black Pacific Ocean. I know there must be thousands of people on the earth below who would give almost everything they own to be in my place at this instant. This is my world; I am the king of my world."

I had no more than finished that thrasonic thought when I was overcome with the feeling of foreboding and caution.

"Watch it. You'd better be checking around. You remember, don't you?"

I removed my feet from the stirrups they had been resting on and sat forward in my seat to begin running a page-by-page check of the ECAM★ to insure all the aircraft systems were functioning properly. Satisfied that they were, I scanned the overhead panel to make sure there were no annunciator lights illuminated. The panel was dark. The cabin pressure was optimal. Every switch was properly positioned. The instruments and radios in the center console that separated me from my first officer were responding accurately to every minute detail within their designed range of operation.

Still not satisfied, I manually tuned my navigation radio to the closest VOR★ station to us, Port Hardy, 112.0 megahertz. It was only a few dozen miles behind us on the north shore of Vancouver Island, Canada, near the mouth of the Queen Charlotte Strait. I listened for the three-letter Morse code identifier, YZT, then compared the VOR direction needle on my RMI★, and its associated DME★ readout, to the moving map display energized on my navigational screen set in the panel directly in front of me. Switching the screen to the three-hundred-sixty degree view while simultaneously selecting the 'VOR' button on the function control panel, I was able to see the electronically created image of the Port Hardy VOR station. It was exactly where it was supposed to be: seventy-two nautical miles behind our tail. We were within one quarter of a mile of where the Inertial Navigation and GPS Computers said we were at that time along the high altitude airway, J523, during our journey to Anchorage. Everything seemed in order.

I sat back in my chair and let out an expansive sigh while still gazing around the cockpit like I was playing a game of 'I Spy.' John, the young man seated to my right, seemed to sense my malaise and closed the manual he was reading on the worktable in front of him and snapped off his light with an unmistakably agitated clearing of his throat.

"What's up?" He inquired as he turned to me.

"Oh, nothing. I was just restless there for a second – tryin' to pretend there was something for me to do." I responded while exhaling deeply.

I wasn't fooling him. We'd been together too long for me to try to hide much of anything. He could tell by my tone of voice that I was concerned about something.

John Paneris was a friend of mine. I have flown with him all over the country both day and night. He invited me to spend Thanksgiving with his sister's family one year in Seattle while we were laying over on a trip. With all six of his little nieces and nephews trying at the same time to impress me as I listened attentively to their fascinating but innocent chronicles of life on the playgrounds of Seattle, it was truly a blessed event.

John's family was traditional Greek. And they enjoyed gathering at the table to share love and laughter and plenty of food, good food; his mother was a wonderful cook. She provided a local Starbucks outlet with scrumptious baked goods for years. Before he began exercising and working out on a regular basis, John had fought quite a battle with excess weight. I could understand why. But still, to me he didn't look Greek. I had always pictured Greek men as being handsomely rugged with black hair and dark eyes, like John Kennedy Jr. John had blond hair and silver blue eyes. Instead of ruggedness he emanated gentleness. But he was quick-minded and very well educated.

He turned away for a second or two, and then he leaned in my direction while smiling and rubbing his chin like a cogitative ape, and attempted to assuage my anxiousness in a mildly condescending but unmistakably comic tone.

"Captain, isn't it amazing – I mean the degree of engineering that goes into these airplanes? The instant anything at all goes wrong with it there's a computer someplace that sends us a message telling us what, where, when, and how much it's going cost you and me to fix it. Don't you think so, Captain, Sir?"

I flashed a huge grin. Feeling the tension beginning to vanish, I thought, *"Isn't that exactly like John?"*

"Yeah. It really is amazing when you think about it. I guess we can either thank or condemn Honeywell for that, huh?" I finally replied as I let go of whatever it was, superstition, or guardian angel that had held me captive. He wasn't finished though.

"How would you feel about calling the girls up? We can turn off all the lights and let 'em look at the stars."

"Yeah. We've got a couple of new and really cute stews tonight. They'd enjoy it." I said.

"So would I." John fired right back.

"Now, now John. You're spoken for already, remember?"

The magnificence of the night sky, viewed while cloaked in total darkness from more than seven miles above a remote region of the earth, is beyond human description. Gazing in only one general direction you can see literally thousands of glowing celestial bodies. The heavens are alive with twinkling lights and blazing rockets that seem to appear from nowhere, flash with intensity, and then die before detonation. The Milky Way sparkles captivatingly in its arc across the Empyrean Theater like a diamond necklace splayed alluringly below the neckline of a beautiful woman in a black velvet evening dress. Constellations that are clearly recognizable from the city on a cloudless night vanish in a boiling cauldron of vacuous ardor. In an instant, I am reminded of the truism spoken by Immanuel Kant in 1781.

"Two things fill the mind with ever increasing wonder and awe, the more often and the more intensely the mind of thought is drawn to them, the starry heavens above me and the moral law within me."

After Anne, Katie, and Veronica had left us to resume their cabin duties among the benumbed travelers, John and I restored the cockpit to its former brightly lit atmosphere and resumed our responsibility of delivering our passengers safely and comfortably to the terminal in Anchorage, Alaska. Leaning back, my boots returned immediately to the elevated stirrups in front of me, and I reached for my coffee cup with a smug satiation not unlike an overweening patriarch.

Glancing out the large window to my left into the black void beyond, my eyes were drawn instantly to a tiny capsule of bright light, a commercial cruise ship miles below us alone on the dark waters of the Queen Charlotte Sound. It was probably bound for some festive Alaskan port - its decks teaming with over-stuffed revelers from the lower forty-eight. Watching it pass slowly behind us, I had a few moments to aggregate the present with the past. Here I was on this beautiful night, sitting securely in my Captain's chair watching the world go by and, by-the-way, making an enviable wage while doing so. It was slightly less than four decades before when my tenth-grade English teacher, Ms. Woodson, an ultra-Existentialist-bleached-blond-liberal from Berkley, startled me out of a similar daydream one afternoon in her class with this stiff admonishment:

"David! Get to work! You'll never make a living sitting on your butt looking out the window."

"Ahhh. Ms. Woodson. Where are you now?" I thought to myself.

As an airline pilot, one has much time to think about such exquisite minutia and reminisce about the past. There'd been so many colorful and unforgettable characters intertwined with my aviation career. Mr. Hillman, of course, was one. Another was Bill Saker.

…Bill was an incorrigible fellow who devoted most of his time to as many young members of the opposite sex in and around Roanoke as he could. His favorite hunting grounds were fairs, carnivals, car shows, and high school parking lots. He would cleverly lure adventure-seeking girls (the looser the better), into his twin-engine Piper Twin Comanche, N8531Y, and fly them down over Smith Mountain Lake southeast of Roanoke, Virginia. He wouldn't go into detail on what he did with them after that, but he seemed to always have a smile on his face.

Bill never missed an opportunity to give me his learned advice when I was only a youngster working for Hillman Flying Service on the weekends washing airplanes and doing odd jobs around the airport. He would patrol leisurely around the field in his wood-grained, light blue Ford Pinto wagon looking for "Pigeons," as he called them, to take for rides. He paused long enough to impart his knowledge of the world to me while I was otherwise immersed in engine grease and metal polish. He would wax pompously while accenting every other syllable with a pointed index finger:

"Dave, never get married. Never date any woman over thirty. Always be honest and fair in your dealings with other people. Don't lie. Always be yourself. And never be afraid to kiss a pretty girl."

Bill was well into his fifties, but he looked much younger. He used to own and operate several massage parlors and beauty shops in the Roanoke area. One warm and humid Saturday night in the mid–1960s, deep into the early morning hours, he purportedly loaded his airplane with several scantily clad young ladies from his harem and buzzed up and down Jefferson Street at treetop height scaring the good citizens into believing the Russians were attacking Roanoke. The FAA authorities wanted to pull his license right then and there, but Bill had a Congressman in his back pocket who would never fail to bail him out of any trouble in which he found himself. From what state the Congressman served as a representative Bill wouldn't admit; however, from that day onward, everyone who knew him, from Hopewell to Hollywood, referred to him as "Wild Bill."

I looked across the console toward my friend; he was busy reading his manual while enjoying one of his mother's homemade delicacies – oblivious to the archival scenes racing through my mind at the time.

I remembered how I tried to talk my father into buying an airplane many years ago after I had earned my Private Pilot's license. Dad loved to fly. He flew PBYs for the Navy during World War II, and he'd said a hundred times before that he would like to own a Piper Colt. But he once told me he never trusted himself with the responsibility of maintaining an airplane mechanically. He was afraid he'd let the maintenance of the airplane go unattended until something would break - leaving his family without a husband and father. I always admired his sense of responsibility that way.

I remembered also the years I spent flying turboprop commuter airplanes around the Central Atlantic region. *Air Virginia*, based in Lynchburg, was one of the many small carriers that sprang into existence in the Eastern U.S. after President Carter deregulated the airline industry in 1978, freeing the major airlines from their essential service duties. *Air Virginia* offered frequent flights to and from smaller cities that had been abandoned by the major airlines. With its two dozen Swearingen Metroliners buzzing day and night along routes such as Washington to Charlottesville and Lynchburg, and Baltimore to Dulles and Newport News, *Air Virginia* carried thousands of otherwise ground-bound passengers noisily to their destinations – nineteen at a time.

A major advantage of a small company like *Air Virginia* was the ability and fervent desire of its employees to gather together and party like there was no tomorrow. Maybe it was because the attrition was so high in those days. Due to the massive hiring rates at the major airlines, we never knew whether or not we'd ever see any one particular acquaintance again after that day. But we had a lot of fun because everybody knew everybody else – sometimes too well. That type of relaxed atmosphere no longer exists in major airlines. I am sure it was lobbied into oblivion many years ago by *BORE (Bureaucrats On Ridiculous Escapades).*

I reached for the flight release on the clipboard next to John's seat to complete a status check over Biorka Island near Sitka. Because of increasing headwinds, we were shy by almost five hundred pounds on the amount of fuel our dispatcher had planned for us to have on board upon passing the VOR. I wasn't worried though; the upper level winds were forecasted to shift in our favor as we proceeded further northward. We were six minutes behind schedule, but the prospect of reclaiming those six minutes and five hundred pounds seemed favorable.

John acknowledged the inconsistency with little more than a casual grunt. His facial expression concealed any pretense of concern, but his eyes repudiated any attempt at disinterest. We both knew the weather station in Anchorage was reporting the ceiling at *CAT II* minimums with mixed snow and dense fog. According to the forecast, the conditions weren't expected to deteriorate, but no aviator has ever seen a weather forecast etched in stone. We wanted all the fuel we could possibly have when we reached the Anchorage terminal area.

I had also noticed that the fuel was slightly out of balance between the two wings. The right main tank indicated almost five-hundred pounds more than the left one. This didn't cause undue alarm, but it did irritate me slightly – like a tiny pebble in my shoe.

Returning the clipboard to its duty station by the center console, I sat back once again in my seat, and my mind trailed yet again to the sudden euphoria that had come upon me only a short while before. Years ago I learned the hard way that when transient euphoria overtakes my conscious mind I had better be on my toes, because something isn't right. Most veteran pilots approach this state of mind more euphemistically: "Fat, dumb, and happy." It happened a few times in my early professional flying career. One particular event on a warm South Carolina night a long time ago stimulates my memory more than others. I turned my face to the window once more, but this time I saw only my ghostly reflection in that black void. I stared at the figure intensely and whispered to myself,

"You do remember."

Chapter Three

The Chicken Hauler

The life of an on-demand cargo pilot could be described succinctly in differing ways, except in sacred locales, depending on your penchant for impecuniousness, or a hand-to-mouth existence. Most sensible men of stature and standing in the community, possessed of cunning business sense, would scoff at the idea of spending their lives accumulating nothing but additional hours of experience to docket in a logbook. The pay is low - when it eventually comes - the hours on duty are ridiculously long and fatiguing, and the aircraft, more times than not, are beset with odious proclivities toward self-mutilation. They can be as Machiavellian as ex-wives.

One late spring night I was returning to my home airport in South Carolina in the company's Beechcraft model 18 Volpar convert. The venerable Twin Beech had more than proved its worth through the years. Born in 1937, the Model 18 was initially designed as an adversary to Boeing's model 247 in the burgeoning but pyrrhonistic airline industry.

Air travel was viewed by the common man in the mid-1930s as a perilous fad soon to vanish from the scene - as did the Conestoga wagon decades earlier. However, newer aircraft being produced by Douglas and Boeing, among others, were much safer than those designed immediately after World War I. And Mr. Beech's model 18 proved to be a dependable twin-engine workhorse. The variant I was flying was a standard model 18E that had been modified by the Volpar Company. Rather than sporting the tail wheel of the original design, this lengthened craft incorporated a nose wheel. So she sat with her twin tail off the ground like a strutting peahen. It was longer than the original model 18 by nine feet. Most importantly, it displayed two 750-shaft horsepower turbine engines produced by the Garrett-Air Research Company, which replaced the older round-motor piston engines. It was marketed as the Beech/Volpar Turboliner, and it served in many distinguishable roles – such as Commuter Airliner and Executive Transport. Its saddle charge this particular night had a more dubious distinction: Chicken Hauler.

Returning home from El Paso, Texas after transporting hundreds of baby chicks to an egg producer near that desert city, "Bev", as I named her, performed flawlessly. She was light, and she responded deftly to every input on her controls. As we flew onward into the night we sailed swiftly past sleepy towns and villages across the southland leaving behind, I imagined, a wistful cadence, beckoning young impressionable children to dream of far away Castalian adventures. We were in harmony – Bev and I. She was purring, and I was singing. There was no better place in the world to be. I was euphoric. Little did I suspect that in just a short time Bev would turn on me like an insufferable Soubrette.

Part Two

On March 4, 1987, at 2:34pm, a Spanish built CASA 212-CC commuter aircraft with twenty-two persons aboard was on its final approach to the Detroit Metropolitan Wayne County Airport's runway 21R. As the aircraft descended through approximately two-hundred feet above ground, it banked to the right, corrected itself, then abruptly rolled somewhere in the neighborhood of ninety degrees to its left. The nose dropped precipitously. It then rolled back to the right causing its right wing to plunge into the ground several hundred feet left of the runway centerline. The aircraft skidded almost four hundred feet into a grouping of parked airport vehicles where it came to rest beneath gate F10 of the terminal building. Fire erupted immediately. Of the passengers and crew aboard, nine lost their lives that day. Seven were seriously injured. Six escaped with minor injuries of varying degrees.

The weather at the airport when the crash occurred was sublime: Light winds out the south – less than ten knots - cool temperatures averaging thirty-eight degrees around the field, good visibility - twenty miles. What could have gone wrong? Among the surviving passengers were two deadheading pilots. Each was commuting to Detroit from Cleveland, Ohio to start their respective flight duties. When questioned about the accident, they both recalled hearing the left engine making an inappropriate but familiar sound just before control of the aircraft was lost. They effectively described the sound as an intermittent growl similar to a car racing its motor rhythmically. To each of them the specific noise was attributed to a propeller moving into and out of the ground-fine pitch, or 'Beta mode,' as it is commonly defined.

A propeller aircraft equipped with jet engines is referred to as a turboprop, or turbo-propeller aircraft. The engines may be either free-spinning turbines, which utilize air pressure developed by the spinning turbine blades to rotate the propeller shafts (much like a child blowing air across a pinwheel to make it spin around), or, as in this particular case, geared.

A geared turbine engine begins spinning the propeller the instant the pilot presses the start switch – like the machinations of that old player piano at the carnival after you've dropped your quarter into the slot. In both examples there are jet engines powering spinning propellers that either pull or push the aircraft through the air. One advantage of geared turbine engines is that they react with immediate positive forward thrust to a forward throttle input. A free-spinning turbine engine may take seconds to develop forward thrust from an identical throttle setting.

Another beneficial aspect of turboprop airplanes, even small personal types, is their ability to reverse the thrust of their propellers, which is utilized after touchdown when landing. By moving the power lever (throttle), the pilot can vary the amount of air thrust either forward or rearward depending on the angle at which the propeller blades are biting the oncoming air. In what is known as the 'Alpha' mode, the pilot moves the power lever, and a mechanical propeller governor changes the angle of the propeller blades. Operating in the 'Beta' mode, the pilot has direct mechanical control over the angle of the spinning propeller blades by again, simply moving the power lever.

To transition from the Alpha range to the Beta range, the pilot merely moves the power lever reward past the flight idle gate. The flight idle gate is a mechanical stop located at the bottom range of travel of the power lever. This gate represents the lowest power setting that can be selected in flight. One could compare that setting to simply removing one's foot from the gas pedal of an automobile while driving down the highway. Pulling the lever up and over the gate further to the rear into the Beta range causes many new and exciting things to happen – especially if the airplane is still in the air.

The official National Transportation Safety Board report of the accident, published many months after the investigation was completed, stated, in part, that the pilot-in-command at the time of the crash had developed a chronic tendency of utilizing the Beta range while still on his short final approach in order to slow his aircraft and lessen the total landing distance. This egregious practice, likened to walking a tightrope suspended above a den of starving lions, should be first on the list of pitfalls to avoid for every prospective turboprop pilot. The consequences are disastrous.

Twin-engine airplanes revel in symmetry. That is to say, the two engines must produce equal amounts of power, so as to unleash the stallion to gallop gracefully through the cislunar heavens like a true winged thoroughbred. If this operating condition is not met, then the craft flies with asymmetric or unequal thrust. With that, it grovels through the air sideways like a vertiginous rabid boar.

Purportedly, the pilot of this doomed craft employed his iniquitous practice one too many times. When he moved the power levers beyond the flight idle gate into the Beta range, whether intentionally or not, the left propeller assembly, which may have been rigged unequally with the right one, began its reverse thrust operation. All symmetry was lost. Worse, one engine was pulling, the other was pushing. Thus, the uncontrolled roll to the left. With less than two hundred feet to recover before diving into the ground, it was all over in about a dozen terrified heartbeats.

It had been a long and exhausting day for me. I had been awake for more hours than I cared to remember. And at three a.m. on this placid night I was more than ready to get Bev back on the ground and into the barn. As I approached the field from the west I purposely did not call the radar approach controller on the radio. During the previous few months he had cogently enticed me into executing what he called the "John's One Approach" when the weather was clear. That meant that anytime I was returning to land after one o'clock in the morning I was not to bother him because he would be asleep. I was to silently approach to within five miles of the airport and then call the tower controller for landing instructions. He never did say, but I automatically assumed his name, whether first or last, was John. Either way it served its purpose.

I called the tower on the radio and was indolently greeted with the same achromatic monotony normally received from mothers-in-law.

"Yeah, uh, cleared to land – runway your choice. Wind is calm, altimeter 30.04, after landing, taxi to the ramp. G' night."

Evidently, we were late to the party.

I flew over the airport and maneuvered Bev around to land to the south, on runway 18. In so doing, we could roll free-and-easy to the end, and I'd have only a short distance to taxi before reaching my company's ramp. With sleep heavy in my eyes, an alluring vision of the recently laundered cotton sheets that I had put on my bed two days before appeared in my mind, and I was getting closer to them by the mile.

Gear down, flaps down, slow to Vref speed, we were almost home. All I had to do now was glide the last couple of thousand feet. At about thirty feet above the runway I reduced power to the flight idle gate.

Suddenly, I was jolted out of my delectable dreamland by a violent roll to the right. Instant paralyzing fear, equivalent to several thousand volts of crippling electrical current, seemed to anesthetize my entire body. There was no time for panic, but that's all I could manage to do. We rolled fifty or sixty degrees. Lights blurred. All sound was silenced. Whether correct or not, I instinctively hauled back on the yoke and attempted to counteract the roll by applying left aileron and left rudder. Conscious thought had already bailed out, and reactive action was all that remained. The roll stopped, but Bev wasn't correcting herself.

Somewhere, sometime, many years before, a wise instructor had drilled into me the redeeming practice of undoing what I had just done if the airplane reacted intolerably to it. I automatically slammed both power levers forward to their maximum power stops. The engines, being the geared type, erupted with power immediately. With corrective action control inputs already set, Bev reacted with eager alacrity.

We leveled out quickly just beyond the edge of the runway - aimed at the sentinel pine trees I knew were out there in the dark. Still shaking, I aligned her again with the runway centerline, reduced power to idle on the left engine, and almost to idle on the right. With that, we plopped down ignominiously with the ruffled scowl of a vexed hippopotamus, 'thump!'

After shutting down on the dimly lit ramp I sat quietly and no doubt numbly for a bit listening to the reprehensibly soft and innocent tinkling of turbine engine exhaust pipes contracting in the cool pre–dawn air. The tower controller, undoubtedly suffering from a narcoleptic episode, was oblivious to the entire debacle. Perhaps he was a graduate of 'John's School of Aloof Observation.'

I logged almost fourteen hours of flying in those two days. And I learned a valuable lesson: Always be ready for the unexpected; it could happen at any moment. Eventually I was able to store the experience in the back of my mind, but a couple of nights went by before I could fully enjoy those clean sheets.

Chapter Four

Beginnings

I performed another enroute check with an implied fix abeam Sister's Island along our new aerial Alaskan Highway, J133. Our progress remained stable in terms of time, and the fuel burn was improving slightly as we became lighter with each passing mile, but the slight imbalance had worsened to indicate an eleven-hundred pound disparity between the left and right main tanks. I didn't like it.

"John, I'm going to cross-feed for a while to balance this out." I said to my first officer as I pointed to the consistent irritant illuminated on the ECAM.

John's nod indicated he concurred with my assessment, and he dropped his laminated checklist between the thrust levers so we wouldn't forget that the crossfeed valve was open.

"You need anything from the back? I think I need another cup of coffee." He adjudicated with a stimulating stretch of his arms.

I glanced down at the quarter cup of cold black coffee in my hand and replied,

"That's exactly what I need right now. Let's go with one cream this time. And while you're back there, see if Veronica has any of those Gingerbread cookies."

He contorted out of his seat and slipped through the door. I was once again alone with my thoughts.

"Gingerbread cookies. I remember when Mom used to bake those."

I let my mind return to the past once again while watching the fuel imbalance slowly correct itself. It would take a little while to do so. In the meantime, I gave some serious consideration to documenting all the memories I had collected over the years. I didn't think it would make much of a story that anyone would be particularly interested in reading. But it would be my life's story. And it would include many wonderfully fascinating people. Then, it struck me:

"You need to write all this down so your grandkids will know what you did before they were born."

Slightly overwhelmed by such a detail oriented proposal, I asked myself,

"Where in the world would I even start?" *"Well, why not start at the beginning?"*

Chapter Five

So Disposed

For many years I was stymied by the question: At what age did I become so monopolized by the lure of aviation? Childhood memories of the constant longing to be near airplanes remain vivid in my mind. It seems that one recounted engram triggers another which was impressed long before. Therefore, to settle the matter, I accept the ethos of having been born into this life so disposed.

One of my father's favorite past times in the quiescence of the mid-1950s while living in Greenville's Mississippi Delta region was to while away the hours on leisurely summer evenings at the municipal airport with his buddies. Dad didn't fly anymore himself. He had given that up after the war in order to fully support his family - as he believed he should. (As time went by I came to admire his sacrifice). Two of his friends owned and operated their own private airplanes, and Dad enjoyed their free-spirited camaraderie. Sometime into my third year of life it became Dad's custom to take me with him on these post-suppertime sorties. He would pack me into the family's two- toned emerald green and white three-holed Buick and trundle me off to the airport to await the arrival of the evening's commercial

DC-3 flight. He kept a sharp parental eye out from the hangar office after depositing me in the grass unabashedly beneath the four-foot chain link perimeter fence segregating the meager parking lot from the airport apron. So affixed, I stood and waited attentively for the first sign of the approaching airliner.

Unbeknownst to me at the time, our town was quite small – existing primarily as an agrarian community. Its isolated and irenic airport was serviced but four times daily by the fledgling airline company, Southern Airways – one of the many regional airlines promoted into operation by the Civil Aeronautics Board shortly after World War II. So, besides the occasional crop duster that would arrive and depart without fanfare, there wasn't much traffic around Greenville's airfield. In fact, some would have said the airport was chronically unemphatic. If I could have understood such a term at my tender age I would have emphatically disagreed. To me it was magical. It was alluring. It was a portal to a thousand untold stories. The concrete runways represented stalwart launching pads to worlds I knew nothing of, but I sensed them just the same.

Pacified by the warmth of the setting sun on my back, I waited patiently and expectantly at the fence for the first distant rumblings of the thunderous round motors of the reliable DC-3s. My budding three-year-old brain conjured up unsullied Cherubic adventures while listening to the peaceful but somehow doleful call of the meadowlarks from across beryline carpets of grass stretching to the distant horizon. There were no seducements from infantine temptations. I was captivated solely by what had been cast before me – and what would shortly arrive. Standing quietly,

I fell into harmonious communion with a beatific presence which, somehow, seemed to unfold a mesmeric runway to decades past. Only the faded windsock floating languidly in the gentle breeze belied the stillness of portraiture. Creation consisted simply of warbling meadowlarks, the far-reaching airfield, the warmth of the sun, and the imaginativeness of a young boy clutching a wire fence in innocent anticipation.

With the acuity of a child awakening with a giddy excitement on Christmas morning, my ears never failed to receive the first modulations of the gathering baritone cannonade that preceded the arrival of the sleekly streamlined Douglas. My eyes fervently scanned castle-laden skies to the distant southwest for the first glimpse of the giant airliner arriving from its storybook kingdom – miles away across a great river. Locking onto its ever-growing silhouette, I guided my homager to the runway with practiced skill and cunning. I memorized every stimulus to my senses when the grand and commanding ship paraded majestically past my vantage point: Its whirling chrome propellers reflected the brilliance of the setting evening sun. Powerful barrel drum engines pounded rhythmically but effortlessly as it paraded stately to its throne at the gate. The left engine slowly unwound to a stop - its propellers frozen at attention. The Captain, hero of the modern ages, confidently tossed his window rearward in order to survey his earthly domain from his lofty perch. The passenger door near the tail, hinged at the bottom, opened – revealing five short steps as it descended to the ground. The agent greeted the hostess with a smile and a friendly wave. She faithfully returned the salutation. Grown up people in hats, and suits, and fancy dresses stepped down and hurried to the diminutive yellow brick terminal building while others, just a few, waited calmly at the fence. With a valet's urbane etiquette, the uniformed agent then signaled his readiness for the boarding of the departing passengers. Smiling and waving goodbye with an unfeigned hospitality, the hostess closed the threshold, and the gleaming airliner was ready to fly again.

I cried as the thundering sunlit transport lifted off, retracted its wheels, and banked gracefully away toward a world I had no conception of. I dared not breathe until I could neither see, nor hear any evidential trace of the object of my cathexis; none could beguile me away.

Dad, being the gentlemanly soft-hearted man he was, gave me a little while alone with my imagination before enticing me to join him for the short journey back to our collective lives together with the family. The familiar scenes were played time and time again before we moved away from Greenville – and Mississippi. However, all that I had gathered in my little mind from those salad days were to play a continuing efficacious role in the years to come.

Chapter Six

On To Houston

My family never lived in any one location for more than about seven years at a time. Dad was transferred from Greenville, Mississippi to Houston, Texas in the middle of 1963. His company, City Steel of Jackson, had opened an office there in order to reap some of the benefits being awarded by NASA's neonate space program underway in Houston. It was Dad's job to research, estimate, and bid on construction jobs at what he referred to as "Nascent NASA" The future of space exploration was clearly located in Clear Lake. The benignancy of Rice University, combined with the openhearted hospitality of Houston's citizenry in the early 1960s, coalesced to foster the creation of what now is as iconic as Mickey Mouse is to Walt Disney. When we when think of NASA, we think of Houston.

The deeply seeded and ever growing desire within me to fly was fertilized almost daily by the frenzied astral environment that defined Houston, Texas in the 1960s. Popular television shows such as 'Lost In Space,' and 'Star Trek,' helped to spur the city and the entire country on to adopt the exhilarating idea of space exploration as the preordained destiny of that generation. Even the airlines, having recently introduced the luxuriousness of jet travel to the public, aggregated the quiet swiftness of jet aircraft with the flourishing magnetism of space.

With monikers for their scintillating gems such as TWA's Star Stream, Eastern's Whisper Jet, and American's Astro Jet, the major airlines hoped to seduce the bourgeoisie into experiencing the thrill and lavish splendor of cross-country air travel. Not to be outdone, the ignoble regional airline, Trans Texas (known locally as Tree Top), jumped on the galactic bandwagon by renaming their venerable, but hopelessly outmoded, piston-powered DC-3s "Super Starliners." However, I doubt if any of the stoic cowboys that boarded them in Waco gave much thought to space travel while riding their bucking broncos through the boiling Texas skies at four-thousand feet to Midland.

While Trish and Bill, my older sister and brother, along with millions of other parturient teenyboppers, were narcotized by the glamorous and fervid lifestyles of hip movie stars and Rock and Roll musicians, I could concentrate on little else but aviation.

Don Fass, a print and electronic media editor who came of age in the 1960s wrote of the time: *"The sixties were an exciting, revolutionary, turbulent time of great social and technological change: Assassination, unforgettable fashion, new musical styles and sounds, Camelot, civil rights, gay and lesbian liberation, a controversial and divisive war in Vietnam, the first manned landing on the moon, mind-blowing scientific discoveries, peace marches, World's Fairs, flower power, great television and film, and unabashed sexual freedoms."*

As a young boy sprinting toward young manhood in early December 1967, I was vaguely aware of the socials upheavals that surrounded me, but I was too far removed from direct participation in them to be swayed politically. My brother and sister were both old enough to form their own thought-provoking opinions about the *supposedly important* issues of the time, but I tended to side systematically with our father on these clinquant topics. I had no idea what 'politically' even meant – nor did I care. I was twelve years old, Christmas was fast approaching, and I was to fly for the first time the very next day.

I awoke well before dawn on December 17th. It was drizzly and foggy in Houston. Spying through the Venetian blinds at the head of my bed, I could follow the cloaking tendrils of mist illuminated by the gas lamp burning near our driveway as it slowly drifted through the large willow trees in our front yard like wandering, forlorn, ghostly apparitions in search of their very souls. It would have been a good day to retreat back under the covers and dream of blue skies and bicycling with my friends. But that thought never entered my mind. The mere presence of such meteorological hindrances as rain and fog could not dampen my festive spirit. I was going to fly.

I jumped excitedly out of bed and ran down the carpeted hall to my parents' bedroom. Their light was shinning under the door; they were up. Duly satisfied, I quickly prepared myself for the day ahead of my mother and me. The shower was but a sparkly flash of water; I'm not altogether sure I even got wet. Then with the utmost in precision and detail, I dressed in the Sunday suit my mother had laid out for me the night before. Traveling by commercial jetliner in 1967 was impressive enough that even the most austere villager was compelled to display at least an improvised attempt at formality. Said simply, people dressed better in those days.

I heard my mother enter the room as quietly as she could. She inspected my appearance with the practiced eye of a platoon leader insuring his troops are adorned properly for battle. In the fashion of June Cleaver, she wanted to ensure her son would be suitably groomed before appearing in public for such an auspicious occasion as this. I laced my polished shoes, combed my hair – making sure to wet my cowlick – and headed back down the hall to breakfast. My brother never stirred; I couldn't understand his insouciance.

Dad drove us to Houston's Hobby International Airport that morning with specific instructions on what we were to accomplish before the day was through. I suppose I heard him talking to us, but I wouldn't have been able to recall what was said during the drive. My mother and I were flying to Greenwood, Mississippi in order to drive my grandparents back to Houston to spend Christmas with our family. My siblings and I were blessed with wonderfully kind Christian grandparents who lived their beliefs in the reposing and quietly secluded Mississippi Delta town of Ruleville, (population 2000), thirty miles to the northwest of Greenwood. Being quite elderly, they were daunted by the prospect of attempting to navigate the sprawling metropolis of Houston; thus our mission that day.

The dewy monochromatic dawn was gradually brightening as we stepped through the sliding glass doors onto the expansive white-tiled floor of the spacious terminal building. The chilling rain had begun in earnest, and the blanket of fog showed no signs of abatement. Dad expressed his concern for the punctuality of our departure with a deepened brow.

"I hope this fog lifts a little before you go."

Mom said nothing, but she continued with doting assiduity to fuss with my cowlick. We approached the attentive, mustachioed ticket agent behind the walnut counter of Delta Airlines with our two suitcases. My mother greeted him with a warm "Good morning," and gave him our itinerary papers. I wasn't much taller than the counter – my eyes being at about countertop height - and I observed every detail of the morning's transaction from my submental position.

From some faraway billet a loudspeaker echoed a man's deep droll voice with an announcement proclaiming the eminent arrival of an airliner that I assumed was quite significant in the grand scheme of things:

"May I have your attention please? National Airlines proudly announces the arrival of flight thirty-seven, DC-8 Luxury Jet service from Los Angeles, now arriving at gate B4."

I had never been to Los Angeles, but I knew there were many rich and famous people living there. I imagined there were movie stars on that very jet – that powerful, four-engine DC-8 with the stylized sun god on the tail. Therefore, I was a little disappointed when I didn't see anyone running impetuously toward gate B4.

The balding agent picked up a telephone receiver and dialed a four-digit number. He wrote down some information on a pad while giving me a serious look, which I interpreted as one of surprised discovery of some egregious error I had committed. I removed my hands from the counter and coyly checked them to ensure they were still clean; they were. Next, he procured two ticket booklets from a slot on his side of the counter and began marking in red ink all the blank boxes with information he gleaned from a large, thick volume that resembled the city Yellow Pages directory. I remember it had the letters 'O.A.B.' on the cover. He continuously changed the position of his head while he was writing – searching for the optimum angle through which to focus his reading glasses. When he finished writing out the tickets he put them both under a rubber stamp machine and stamped them several times in various places. He then took our two bags, tied blue and white destination tags on them, and then sent them off on the black conveyor belt that disappeared into the wall behind him. He stapled the stubs to our ticket jacket, and then he proceeded to explain to my mother what all the numbers and letters in the boxes meant.

I, having long since lost interest in numbers and letters, let my gaze wander down the long bank of ticket counters of the different airlines that served Houston: Braniff, Eastern, Continental, TWA, Pan Am – there were so many. People were standing, talking, gesturing, approaching, and departing with purpose. My dad was doing pretty much the same as I was while whistling along with a Frank Sinatra song wafting rhythmically from the terminal's public address system. It was a new song that Dad liked – something about strangers in the night…. Dad whistled when he could let his mind wander; although, I assumed he was more interested in numbers and letters than I was.

We finished what we needed to do at the counter and headed down the corridor toward our gate – B1. Hobby airport had three concourses that fingered off the terminal like you would spread fingers on your hand. The 'B' gates were in the middle concourse. I was in a hurry to see the planes parked on the apron, but Mom wanted to browse through the gift shop. I almost let my disappointment show, but then I remembered the neat model planes the gift shop sold. So, we spent a little time there. Dad said we had thirty minutes before the flight left anyway.

In 1967, our country was still fairly isolated from the domestic troubles in the rest of the world. Dad said that a man's word was honored as the truth to a fair degree. Islam, along with (what I was beginning to believe) its cancerous, satanic beliefs, was largely viewed as somewhat of a novelty – not to be taken seriously, and certainly no threat to us. So, airport security was practically non-existent. In fact, I don't remember seeing even one police officer that morning.

Mom purchased her magazine to read on the flight, and then we strolled eagerly to gate B1 to board our plane. If not for the rain I would have climbed the outside steps to the observation deck that ran the length of the concourse roof. It offered several telescopic viewers that emanated a soft ticking sound when you dropped a nickel in the slot. I had enjoyed many sunny days up there with Dad watching arriving and departing planes. It was a popular place for families to spend leisurely Sunday afternoons dreaming of exotic destinations.

My mother and I stepped up to the turnstile, just like the ballpark, and she handed the agent our tickets. Dad put his hand on my shoulder and admonished me to ensure that my mother did not get lost on the return drive to Houston later in the week.

"Dave, I want you to make sure your mother doesn't take the wrong road on the way back. You watch out for that, okay? And make sure she calls me when you get to Ruleville."

"Okay, Dad. I will."

The young agent gave each of us an umbrella for the short walk to the plane, and out we went. The white DC-9, tinseling in the rain-stratumed floodlight, was parked at an angle to the concourse - its polished aluminum stairway descending into the refluent concrete. I could see the hostess standing just inside the doorway ready to welcome us on board as we climbed the many steps. New sights, sounds, and smells bombarded my senses. From the tail of the plane I heard a small jet engine whining softly with great volumes of heated air rushing out of some distant, sibilatory exhaust port - joined by a chorus of ear-piercing hydraulic and electric motors. The distinctive fetor of jet fuel was permeating the air all around. As we neared the top step I could see the pilot through his side window reading his checklist as he reached for a switch overhead. Water cascaded down the glass in undulating silver waves.

Stepping inside the foyer, I detected an earthy aroma - an amalgamation of jet fuel, plastic - like a Slip N Slide - fresh coffee, and human exudation. The hostess greeted us warmly and ushered us to our seats – 2A and B. Somehow she knew this was my first airplane ride. She knelt slightly and pinned a set of Delta Airlines wings on my lapel and told me I would remember this day forever. After fastening my seat belt I turned my face to the window beside me and kept it there. The distant motors stopped and started with irregular frequency.

The rain was coming down even harder than before, and I couldn't see more than a few hundred feet. Intrigued,

I watched the last passenger to board come bounding energetically up the steps with a shotgun case in his hands. He shook the rain off of himself with vigor as he smiled for the hostess. Tossing the case in the overhead rack, he fell back with casualness into the seat across the aisle from my mother, nodded a polite salutation to her, asked the hostess for a cup of black coffee, and then opened his newspaper. He wasn't excited at all. This I did not understand.

I heard the heavy boarding door on the other side of the partition close with a sturdy metallic thud. Then the stairway lifted itself to parallel the ground and retracted into a bay beneath the floor of the plane. The hostess picked up a black telephone receiver and spoke briefly to someone, and then she strolled through the cabin smiling at everyone with conversant eyes.

I could barely hear the engines increasing their clamorous shrill as we began to taxi away from the terminal across the fog-shrouded airfield. We bumped along, making several turns, first one way and then the other, while the hostess explained the necessary safety features and procedures on board through the P.A. system. The rain continued to run down my window in rivulets as I watched starred white, blue, red, green, and amber lights, strung like pearls, each color sharing its own secret with the pilots up front, disappear into the mist. It seemed like we roamed for miles in a strange mythological world. Finally, we reached our takeoff runway and stopped.

There was a roadway nearby, and I could see cars pass through the obscuration as their headlights scribed dancing patterns in the water on the window. After a few moments the pilot announced his readiness for takeoff. I glanced at my mother.

"Here we go, Dave. Are you ready?" She asked.

"Yes." I told her. My fingers gripped my armrests in sensitized anticipation.

We lined up on the runway – the misty headlights behind us someplace. Then with a cacophonous grinding roar, the engines, many feet behind us, erupted into a unified single-minded power. My memory instantly recalled the day my father and I walked unaware around the corner of a fence at an automobile junkyard years before and were intercepted by two male Dobermans chained to a steel post in the ground. Their truculent snarls, intensified by blood-choking strains against their collars, mixed into a single-minded exigency to tear us into very small pieces. Sudden unleashed power is quite impressive.

I was forcefully pushed back into my seat by the acceleration. This was fantastic! The rain on my window began streaking to the rear instead of down. We gained speed quickly – the bright runway lights flashing past with ever increasing swiftness until they were mere streaks of white light. As the nose of the plane lifted, I felt the pressure on my back increase - like a ride on the *Tilt-A-Whirl* at a carnival. There was a surprising final bump from the bottom of the plane, and then it became as smooth as glass. We were simply hanging, suspended in mid-air as the runway dropped away from us. Still pinned in my seat, I watched a section of the terminal pass beneath us before we were engulfed by a thick gray void. I looked again at my mother. She smiled and patted my hand. It was going to be a great day.

Adults, especially older ones skilled in the art of social subterfuge, enjoy spying on children, especially younger ones who, having been thrust into settings requiring cerebral affectations of a more urbane nature, seem to brandish newly- found cosmopolitan mores as easily as they do skinned knees. Children know when things are different. And they sense when they need to behave differently than they normally do. When Mommy and Daddy are dressed in their Sunday best and acting more polite than they do at home, little Tommy, also dressed in his finest, will be on his best behavior. Perhaps there is truth to the proverb: "The saddle makes the horse."

As we rocketed up through the misty stratum I could no longer hear the engines behind us. The only evidence of motion was an increasing rush of friction-heated air just inches from my nose. I sat back in my seat and looked at my mother reading her magazine. She returned my gaze with a smile of understanding. Our hostess, who had begun serving our breakfast, then captured my attention. She worked efficiently and quickly.

There were only three passengers in the section we were in, so she could dote over each of us a little longer. After she spread a white linen tablecloth on the pull-down tray in front of me, I unwrapped my silverware and laid them aside without clanging them together. Then I draped the napkin across my lap. I answered, "Coke, please" when she asked what I would care to drink. The hostess then poured my mother a cup of coffee and placed it on the saucer in front of her. Shyly, I found that I was dividing my time between the enticements outside the window and the physical endowments of our hostess.

At twelve years of age, I was beginning to notice pretty women – even if they were many years my senior. She had shoulder length auburn hair that framed one side of her slender face. And her eye-catching short uniform skirt did little to hide the fact that she was a female….

Soon, before me lay an attractive breakfast of quiche, fresh fruit, and a blueberry muffin. I wanted to impress her with my table manners. So, eating slowly, I tried very hard not to spill anything on the clean linen cloth, nor on me. Mom, whether or not aware of my obvious display of gossamered concupiscence, approved of my obvious display of table manners; she was watching. Outside, the sky began to take on a lighter hue. And in just a few moments I was treated to the most spectacular sight I had ever seen in all my twelve years.

Before driving away from the house that morning, Dad had mentioned something about the tops of the cloud layers. He said he hoped that we would climb up on top of the clouds so I could see them from above. Comparing the experience to a few films I had seen, he tried to communicate the effect to me; I couldn't quite grasp the mental visualization. When I actually witnessed the breathtaking scene for myself, I was without words.

The gray mass, becoming lighter each second, began to break apart – allowing glimpses of blue and pink and orange to filter in through my window. We were slipping through the wisps with blinding speed. Suddenly we broke free into the clear sunny sky, and I found myself skimming rapturously along on the top of a quilted canopy. Playfully surfing the billows like a winged dolphin, the dark shadow of our jet raced with us. Bubbling volumes of cotton candy clouds, edged in pink and blue, whisked past rapidly, and I imagined myself stepping out and running up and down their beckoning slopes. They seemed friendly somehow. I even imagined kids my own age standing atop them waving to us as we flashed past. Gradually the frothy carpet fell away as we continued climbing higher and higher into the brilliantly blue sky – far above the gloominess that suppressed the earth below.

Part Three

Almost five decades have passed since that phenomenal day, and I have flown more than six million miles in those years. As all of us in my generation have witnessed, the genteelness in society, as well as in commercial aviation, has long since been usurped by a dysphemistic litany of rude, narcissistic behavior and speech. Evidently, the prophesies in the Bible are apodictic; we are headed in the direction we were destined to travel.

The day passed much too quickly. After changing planes in Jackson, Mississippi, my mother and I touched down on the sunlit runway in Greenwood at around four o'clock aboard a tired-looking Southern Airways Martin 404 and were graciously received by my grandparents at the wire fence of the small country airport a few miles east of town. My grandmother was attired in a light blue formal, patrician print dress. Granddad, sporting his unimpeachable grey coat and red tie, pendulated his walking stick in his characteristic statesmanlike manner – always the true Southern gentleman. The weather had cleared, and the sun warmed the plowed cotton fields surrounding the airport. We were the only two passengers to complete their journeys in Greenwood that balmy afternoon. Of course, Granddad wouldn't drive away until after the plane took off – so I could watch it go.

I remember that day just like the pretty Delta hostess said I would. It is engraved in my memory like etchings in stone. It was joyous, exciting, and peaceful – all at the same time. It also rekindled a spirit that I knew was inside of my soul. Flying was for me. No matter what it took, no matter what it cost, I would begin my pursuit of a career in aviation as soon as I could. Mom and Dad both knew of my passion, and they encouraged me in every way they knew how. With a poignant committedness, I watched the inveterate Martin fade away into the northeastern horizon toward Oxford – its next stop. It would be almost three years before I would fly again.

Chapter Seven

Where's Roanoke?

One of my top ten favorite films of all time is the 1959 Alfred Hitchcock thriller, North By Northwest. Sinister foreign spies hot on the trail of a U. S. government agent mistake the leading man, Roger Thornhill, a New York advertising magnate - played by the dashing, well-tailored, Cary Grant - for the elusive and non-existent decoy, George Kaplin. In the third scene, strong-armed hoods in the employ of the malevolent caitiff, Phillip Van Dam, kidnap Thornhill and abscond with him to a safe house in Long Island's exclusive Glen Cove district. While a captive there, Roger Thornhill attempts to persuade the errant 'Simon Legree' that he has committed a dreadful misdeed by mistaking his true identity with the heretofore unseen Mr. Kaplin. Later the same night, Thornhill shrewdly escapes the clutches of the hangman, and the story of intrigue and espionage begins to unfold. In the blink of an eye Roger Thornhill's life was forever changed. Perhaps one reason I enjoy this movie so is because it directly reflects how our own lives can change just as suddenly – with no warning signs. In December of 1968, my family would experience another precipitous life-changing event.

Dad came home from work one evening in late October, and as we sat down to dinner he said he had some important news for us. Maybe there was something solicitous about his manner of voice, but my brother and sister looked at each other with dread. They were both in high school, so they probably thought Dad had made plans for a "fun-filled" family vacation at Yellowstone National Park or some other educational venue the next summer.

"City Steel has been bought by the Ingalls Iron Works Company in Birmingham." He announced. We looked plaintively at each other – expecting his next pronouncement to be we would be moving to Birmingham, Alabama.

Dad and Mom married shortly after World War II, and Dad entered the prestigious Colorado School of Mines in Golden, Colorado. After graduating he found work in the steel business as an engineer and draftsman. As in many companies, if he wanted to advance through the echelons he would be required to relocate from time to time.

"They are transferring us to Roanoke, Virginia. I need to be there in two weeks to begin putting a plant into operation."

I was about to ask where Roanoke was when Trish moaned a gut-wrenching sob, stood up, and ran from the table in tears. Bill laid his fork down dejectedly – his mouth twisted in painful resignation. He stood and quietly followed his sister down the hall to her room. Mom, already informed of the news, turned to Dad and said,

"Oh Sandy, this is not going to be easy."

She excused herself and went to console her two older inconsolable children. Dad sat silently at the head of the table staring vacuously out over the roast beef and potatoes. I knew he was feeling like the bad guy. Trish was in her senior year of high school. She was very popular at

Bellaire High – active in several clubs and having different dates on Friday and Saturday nights. Bill was emerging as the entourage leader in his social circles. He wore bell-bottom jeans and wire-rimmed glasses, owned every Beatles album produced up to that time, and believed his little brother to be a pestiferous irritant. Moving away to another state at this pivotal point in their lives would be devastating.

I remained contemplative for a few moments until Dad shook his head slowly and grunted in confoundment. Then I looked him in the eye and eagerly asked,

"Where's Roanoke?"

Virginia…. Virgin Islands…. Venus…. At the time they impressed me as being equidistant from Houston. I'd never met anyone from Virginia. My school friends were no help either. They mentioned names like Walter Raleigh, Thomas Jefferson, James Madison, and Grover Stump. In our insensate pre-adolescences, we all agreed that everyone in Virginia paraded majestically in white wigs, addressed each other as "the gentleman from…," and would never allow Robert E. Lee to abdicate his position as the monarch. By the time moving day finally arrived I was convinced we were about to enter a world devoid of television, indoor plumbing, and was as anachronistic as the dress my sister wore to the previous year's prom.

Dad packed up his essential things and headed northeast for Roanoke four weeks before we did. He wanted us to stay in school to finish the fall semester. Mom insisted he take our two mixed-breed dogs, George and Jim, because one: They couldn't ride more than ten miles before throwing up all over the back seat. And two: She wasn't about to travel one thousand miles in a stinky 1965 Ford Galaxy 500 with two pertinacious teenagers, (especially in the days before i-pods and computer games), a youngster who only wanted to FLY to Virginia, not DRIVE, and two dyspeptic pooches possessed by the annoying habit of barking at every large truck we passed. Mom was a saint, but she did not inherit the patience of Job.

We spent the last night in our house on Holly Street in Spartan conditions. A few of my friends – Mark, Sammy, Kerry, Denzial, and his younger brother Gary, came over with sleeping bags to 'camp out' in the living room. The movers had carried away almost everything in the house that day. Trish and Bill, loath to see their rooms so featureless, spent the night with their friends for one final hurrah. As my sister drove away, still in tears, I thought of Jephthah's daughter in Judges, chapter eleven – a bittersweet end…. The next day, Saturday, we loaded up the Ford, said goodbye to our friends and neighbors who had gathered in the cold to see us off, and mournfully headed for Mississippi where we would spend Christmas with our grandparents before continuing on to Roanoke. We were on our way; to what we had no idea.

It was always good to be with Gramma and Granddad; however, they could see the ennui displayed in our countenances. The gray winter matched our mood of aimless isolation. For the first time that I could remember we had no home. Houston was gone forever, and Roanoke was only an incognizable enigma still lurking over the horizon. Being together gave us some comfort, but we each felt like a downtrodden vagabond. We spoke often of the feeling. It was also the first Christmas I had ever spent without Dad, and I missed his steadfast spirit. Mom was anxious to be on her way, and she decided to leave the day after Christmas.

Granddad insured we had new tires for the trip, and after our somber goodbyes we set out on that bone-chilling dismal morning. The two-lane concrete highways and small penurious towns of the Mississippi Delta were deserted as we made our way north to Memphis. No one wanted to be out in such funereal conditions. Remaining quiet as we drove, we sensed the balefulness. Leaning my head against the rear seat window, staring across a vapid continuum, the endless furrows of the muddy fields raced along like picket fences. They reminded me of the ratcheting slap of a baseball card against the spokes of my bicycle as I peddled with my friends to the donut shop near our home in Houston. But even my imagination could not for long distract my heart from its anxiousness. We were in desperate need of some spontaneous joviality. And it came that night.

At around six o'clock in the evening, deep in the heart of frozen middle Tennessee, Mom proclaimed exhaustion and instructed us to keep a keen eye out for a motel in which to spend the night. We also needed a service station; the gas gauge showed less than one quarter full.

Much of the nation's Interstate Highway system had been only recently completed by 1968, so there wasn't much to choose from in the way of accommodations. We exited lonely I-40 up a rural ramp well after dark. The sky remained overcast, but the deep snow covering the ground reflected what little light there was. A battered road sign on a crooked post rocking gently in the wind pointed the way to Dickson, Tennessee. Mom steered the car left, and we crossed back over the highway onto a blacktop country lane. Descending into snow-blanketed fields and ominous forests that seemed to close in all around us, the ghostly scene reminded me of Sleepy Hollow and Ichabod Crane. Occasionally we would pass a clapboard farmhouse burning a dim light through a drawn window shade. I knew as sure as anything that if we ran out of gas I was going to witness the Headless Horseman come galloping around a bend on that hobgoblin highway screaming insanely and bent on my demise. I moved inward to the middle of the backseat. This was a more 'comfortable' position from which to hear the car's motor if it began gasping for fuel. Thankfully, after several tense minutes, we finally spotted the lights of civilization ahead. With relieved sighs we escaped the haunted forest and entered the hamlet of Dickson.

Growing up with my brother taught me to be resilient as well as redoubtable. Bill loved to pick, and antagonize, and joke, and swagger. I guess you could say he was a genuine hoyden if there ever was one. It was not until I had reached my fifth birthday that I learned his name was not "Bill Don't." However, my sister, bless her soft heart, never learned to counter his shenanigans before she became completely flustered and stormed out of the room. Bill could manipulate her like an Austrian marionette. Actually, it would have been funny had I not so often been on the receiving end of his prankishness myself.

We checked into the Best Western motel in Dickson, located our two rooms – one for Mom and Trish, the other for Bill and me - washed our hands and faces, then crunched across the quadrangle toward the beckoning orange neon lights that rimmed the brick café. Thrilled by the snow, we couldn't resist throwing a few snowballs at each other. But, as usual, Bill went too far and smacked Trish in the face with a slush ball.

"Bill!" She yelled. Then in the same breath she implored, "Mom!"

"Bill, you behave!" Mom reprehended. She had had enough bickering for one day.

Seated in the restaurant, we ordered our supper then passed the time conversing about one thing and another – mostly the drive that day. One of the employees on duty – a young man who appeared to be close to Trish's age, noticed my sister when we came in. With her long straight blond hair and blue eyes, Trish attracted suitors wherever she went. The young man snapped out of his reverie – his eyes locking onto her like a bird dog on a quail when she sauntered through the door. Mom noticed the attention she was commanding immediately. It didn't take long for Trish to notice either. Maybe she was looking back. But then, like gasoline trickling toward a flame, Bill noticed. And, true to form, he began teasing her about it at once. First, he threatened to bring the young man over to introduce the two. He voiced his opinion about what their children would look like. Trish, feigning indifference, embarked upon a noological pilgrimage through the depths of the 'Dave Clark Five' repertoire. She was not about to condescend to his juvenility. She wasn't fooling him though, and he knew it. Next, he decided that farm boys from Tennessee would never like girls with big feet – strong teeth maybe, but never big feet.

"Bill, that's enough." Our mother warned. What we didn't know at the moment was that Trish had been sitting all this time with her right foot tucked securely up under her left leg on the chair. I never understood how girls could sit comfortably that way; perhaps it was fashionable in 1968….

The food arrived in time to stave off open warfare; a truce was called. Bill's mouth was occupied with his cheeseburger and fries for a short while, but Trish never changed her posture. Later, between the entrees and the desserts, Bill renewed his vexatious attack. Rethinking his former opinion, he decided big feet or not, the young man and Trish were going to meet, date, fall in love, marry, and summarily produce children with predictably prodigious podiums. That did it! Trish was incensed.

"Bill, you are such a child!" She shrieked. "I don't have to sit here and listen to this."

Quickened by anger, she whipped around in her chair, planted her left foot firmly on the tile floor, stood on it defiantly, and pushed herself away from the table in moral victory as she pulled her right foot off the chair. In its moral truth the Bible warns thee: "Pride goethe before a fall." How wise it is to heed the lessons in Proverbs.

Every eye in the room was fixed on my sister in her moment of triumph. Women everywhere were applauding her feministic insuperability. Declare victory for the weaker sex! With her pert nose in the air and her eyes on the door, she bayoneted her right foot deeply into the doughy depths of mortal horror. I watched the scene unfold in vivid slow motion. Her eyes widened in amplified realization, their plucked brows elevated. Her head reeled from the electric shock coursing through her body. Her ascendant smirk retracted into a terrorized gape. White skin flushed with paralytic fear. Hands and arms flailed wildly for stability, and found none. Then to ensure she had captured the full attention of everyone in the room, just before becoming prostrate she bayed the howl of death. Alas, her right foot was fast asleep.

To this day I don't believe I have ever cast my eyes upon such a rich shade of crimson. Mom had much more consoling to do that night. Bill was to be grounded for a week – whenever we found a place from which to do so. However, my sister was not mollified by his sentence. She wanted him crucified! Give us Barabbas…!

Chapter Eight

Keeping Things Straight

As rational gregarious beings, we often wonder what other people think of us. My wife, who gave up on me long ago, thinks of me as a soporific personality with an acute inertness ad-infinitum impulsion. You know, the urge to do nothing and work hard at maintaining it? It's not easy being a slacker. Truly, a fainéant must expend great amounts of energy to make others think he is doing something important. I suppose I dabbled in the callidity of stealthy skulking by carefully observing the practiced art of truancy by my older brother, Bill. He was a master by any swagman's standards.

It didn't take us long to settle into a routine after relocating to Roanoke, Virginia. On my mother's birthday of 1969, February 8, we moved into our four-bedroom brick house in Sugar Loaf Farms on the outskirts of the city. Our new address was 4849 Brookwood Drive SW. We had a sloping backyard with a stand of woods at the bottom. I had my own bedroom. We even had a basement. I remember how cool it was down there in July, as not many of the homes were built with central air conditioning in those days. The summertime temperatures soared into the nineties. And with the high humidity levels, Dad quickly grew impatient with the sweltering heat. By early August of that first summer we were enjoying central cooling.

Ineffable months passed. New alliances were formed; new enemies were targeted. Life didn't seem drastically different in Roanoke than it had been in Houston. One of my fondest memories of the period is of me sitting at my Black Walnut captain's desk doing my homework while listening to the Woodrum Airport traffic on a small air-band radio that Dad gave me for Christmas. Piedmont Airlines was the primary carrier in Roanoke. The post- war airline had been profitable through the years, and it serviced Roanoke with fifty-eight flights a day. They operated Boeing 727 and 737 jets in addition to large turbo-prop airplanes to destinations throughout the mid- Atlantic region. By referencing the schedule booklets that they published monthly, I knew the type of aircraft and the destination of each flight as it called the tower for takeoff clearance.

By the second summer, at age fourteen, I was ready to begin earning money for flying lessons. I was growing impatient with model airplanes; I wanted the real thing. Moreover, because Dad was the manager at Blue Ridge Steel Company where they fabricated, painted, and shipped various "I" beams and angles with which to build skyscrapers and bridges, Bill and I had summer jobs available whenever we desired them. So, when the sun set on the day that ended my eighth year in school, I asked Dad if I could go to work. He said Bill and I both could start the following Monday.

Dad, Clyde W. Sandidge, was a man's man – a real John Wayne, and not one to be trifled with. At six feet, three inches tall, and two-hundred forty pounds, he was a very imposing figure to any potential adversary. But Dad had one major flaw that betrayed his embodiment of a colossus in a tie. He was blessed with beautiful sea-blue eyes that could radiate such kindness that it was practically impossible to resist the urge to hug him like a favorite teddy bear on cold winter's night. However, at age fourteen I didn't dare entertain such a thought. It would have broken the timeless code of manly independence – whatever that is.

In this first summer at Blue Ridge Steel Company, my brother and I were assigned the task of cleaning and painting a large abandoned upstairs storage room in a section of the three- story decrepit brick building that was to house a new industrial copy machine - the type that draftsmen used back then to copy blueprints. We walked into a dilacerated ghost town littered with bottles and broken glass, a repelling cornucopia of moldy, fly-infested garbage, and a plaguing laminate of mephitic oily grime from many decades of undisturbed deposition. That's what we faced. It was quite a daunting deputation for two teenage boys who had better things to do with their time than work. Nonetheless, after a few days we began to get used to it.

Bill, three years my senior, had long before discovered Dad's true benevolence hiding beneath a mask of vetted surliness. Don't get me wrong. He never attempted to challenge our father face-to-face; that would have resulted in instant death. There was a limit to Dad's accordance. However, the hubris of youth is seemingly omniscient. Bill well knew what he could and could not get away with.

He also knew it would have been treasonous for any self-respecting teenage boy not to seize an opportunity to pull off something he knew better than to do. So on an unseasonably cool and rainy summer morning after rising much too early from a night out with friends, Bill decided a few hours of needed sleep would be much more beneficial to his social life than the inspiring satisfaction of knowing a job, unpleasant as it was, had been well done. What I did not realize in my inchoate adolescence was that Bill, evermore the altruist, had plans for me, too. I was to be the lookout while he pursued his sluggardly appetence.

Standing between two opposing forces is never pleasant. And, more often than not, that's where I would unmindfully find myself. Once, in the seventh grade, among the rest of the budding pubescent postulants, the class was having much difficulty in the reading aloud of a passage of English prose because, it contained the titillating word, "suck." The hapless author could just as well have inserted a brick wall behind the word then quit while he was ahead. One by one, my fellow students failed to surmount the formidable escarpment. The very approach to the word "suck" brought snickers and giggles to the entire room. Exasperated, Ms. Brewer turned to me with her characteristic poise and requested with much felicitousness that I read the paragraph so we could finish the story and move on. What did she understand about me that I didn't? I could have been a hero in the eyes of my classmates. Legends would have been born in the cafeteria for months afterward. All eyes were on me, and you could have heard a pin hit that floor. But what did I do? Without so much as a quiver from the corners of my lips I pronounced the word "suck" with such deliberate aplomb that I could have passed as Walter Cronkite on the CBS Evening News reporting on dire events in the nether regions of Lower Zimbabwe. When I finished reading there was not one sound from the class; they were shocked by the traitor in their midst.

Bill waited strategically for Dad to make his routine appearance in our dingy oubliette. It was Dad's custom to check on us after the morning steam whistle signaled the beginning of the workday. (*Somehow, I seemed to develop a habit of starting out the morning thinking about that old song about Casey Jones*). He made sure we knew just what needed to be done and had procured all of the necessary accoutrements with which to accomplish the day's assignment. After Dad left us with his thundering command, "Y'all get to work," Bill glared at me menacingly and gave me a stern warning:

"I'm going across the breezeway to the 'A' building. If Dad comes back tell him I went to get some stir sticks and drop cloth."

And with that, he slinked down the dark hall to the covered walk bridge leading across the alley to the abandoned office building's second floor. I couldn't imagine where he would find a place to lie down and sleep, because the derelict building, constructed in 1914, was caked in pigeon droppings, dirt, broken glass, and it smelled of musty, rotting wood. Besides, there were rats running around everywhere; I knew because I had already explored all three floors of the macabre fortress. There was nothing in there I would even touch – except maybe with the soles of my boots. However, there was one time when I found a Playboy magazine from the late 1950s up in the attic. That was the first time I had seen a naked woman, other than

Native African women with elephant bones in their noses in the National Geographic, Marilyn Monroe. I was boyishly mesmerized by her firmly rounded breasts and curvy hips. I guess I'd never given women much serious thought before. I'd had a couple of crushes on girls in Junior High School, but I didn't know what to do about it. With a heightened but somewhat shocked awareness, I gave her an approving nod.

What was even more tantalizing were the cars pictured in the advertisements from that era. They were all so round and friendly looking – just like most of my friends' mothers…. Anyway, replaying the scenes of effluent filth in my mind, I couldn't imagine lying prone anywhere in that spider-crawling bat cave. To me it seemed the easiest thing for Bill to do would be to get home earlier and get to bed so he wouldn't be so tired when he got to work. But what did I know? He was seventeen, and he had two beautiful girlfriends.

Dad never did come back to check on us. He was dealing with an errant overhead crane which had also decided that abscondence is more rewarding than accountability. So with daydreams of flying into faraway, exotic lands dancing in my mind's eye, I scraped flaking paint and greasy dirt from windows and moldy brick walls until the twelve o'clock whistle.

———◆◉✦◉◆———

Lunchtime at Blue Ridge Steel Co. was truly a prosaic affair. With only thirty minutes to eat, one needed to be thrifty as well as quick. When the whistle blew, you grabbed your brown-bag meal, secured a reasonably comfortable position in which to relax, and then you ate hurriedly so you could stretch out for a few minutes in a shady place before resuming the day's work of grinding and welding steel beams and angle iron.

Most of the men were quiet and pensive at lunchtime. I suppose several of them often wondered just how they came to be employed in such positions. Where did their dreams end and reality begin? These were not educated men for the most part. Quite a few of them had criminal records of varying degrees of severity. Hard drinkers, tough talkers, but predominately honest and dedicated husbands and fathers defined the majority. With names such as Firebaugh, Whitehead, and Craighead – names that had been honed for two centuries through tempering fire in the Appalachian region of Southwestern Virginia, these men courageously surrendered their lives to the responsibility of supporting and loving their wives and their children. Many couldn't even spell responsibility, but they instinctively accepted it. Dad had an admiring respect for the men who worked for him. Through time, Bill and I both learned also to respect their stoic consecration.

My brother and I were blessed with a mother who cared enough for her family that she would rise early in the morning and prepare our midday meals for us to take to work. Chicken sandwiches, Vienna sausages, chips, and chocolate pudding; these were our favorites. Every day she would, without condition, see to it that we had enough to eat.

As I bounded down the stairs to Dad's office to eat lunch, I wondered how my brother was doing. I felt assured there was no way he would miss out on break time. Dad was quietly devouring his sandwich with huge manly bites while reading through his mail when Bill came stumbling through the doorway. He wordlessly reached for his lunch bag, and then fell back disheveled into the green leather office chair he claimed was his alone at lunchtime.

It was evident he had not groomed himself in the bathroom mirror before entering, because his hair possessed the tousled Rip Van Winkle flair. His eyes also belied his best efforts to express any degree of animation. With an expansive sigh he opened his sack and began to eat in confused cogitation. About then I seriously considered moving into the adjacent office to eat lunch with Dave Burke, the plant's assistant manager, because I was well aware of the volcanic pressure beginning to rumble in Dad's office while Bill sat there stupidly - like a dazed giraffe in a thunderstorm. He was directly in the line of fire. I was sure Dad, the growling bear, would pounce at any moment. In his no-nonsense style, Dad lowered his head and bored over the top of his black-rimmed glasses with steel blue eyes and bellowed at my brother with all the virility of the pride leader, "Bill, what have you been doing?"

Through our years of growth and erudition we learn to associate certain facial expressions with particular circumstances of one's present sociological standing. For instance, the look of joy on a person's face could be compared to the expression a professional baseball player would beam after winning the final game in the World Series. Or, it could be the same expression Julie Andrews exhibited in the movie *The Sound of Music* when she vaulted ecstatically up the stairs after Captain Von Trapp apologized and asked her to stay.

One could just as readily associate the look of sorrow and broken heartedness with the loss of a friend or loved one, like the fractured countenance Mary Stuart Masterson so expertly characterized in the film *Fried Green Tomatoes* when her best friend passed away from cancer. In each case facial expression says more than words ever could.

It was no different this day in Dad's office. Dad's inculpative arrow had caught Bill completely off guard. I thought the end was at hand. I was speechless, so was Bill. When he cast a beseeching glance at me he had the exact same look of helpless resignation Wiley Coyote would cast when the entire cliff was about to crash onto his head. His ears were drooping. I could see the ominous shadow becoming darker with each foot closer the crag got to him. But I didn't have the heart to laugh; somehow I thought I was in trouble, too. After collecting himself as quickly as he could, Bill rushed into the emergency extradition mode. He had to think of something immediately to appease the panting giant. He snatched what viable thoughts he could from the swirling semi-conscience malaise that was his brain. And meaning to say, "straightening things up', he blurted,

'Ugh, just keeping things straight."

In utter astonishment I lowered my head, closed my eyes, and waited for the inevitable atomic blast to send us to Heaven. The passing seconds pounded in my ears like sledgehammers on an iron rail. After several moments of deafening silence in the room, I peeked up sheepishly at Dad. He quietly continued to read the letter he had opened and finished the last of his chicken sandwich with much contented approval. Had he heard Bill's bungled reply? Was he listening to that abominable elucidation? Bill and I looked at each other in amazed perplexity, but we did not say another word. Dad glanced in feigned deference at the rest of the correspondence on his desk then arose to make his noontime rounds of the plant. He had almost passed through the doorway when he stopped. Turning toward Bill to speak with the sanguine temper of a pastor gently admonishing his flock, he said,

"Bill, I want you to come home earlier tonight and get to bed. You need more sleep so you can do your work." Without another word he walked away.

My brother and I have spoken many times of those long summer days we spent at Blue Ridge Steel Co. – that one in particular. We learned about work and we learned about life. We learned most of the time we'd rather be somewhere else. Nevertheless, those paychecks on Friday afternoons made us feel pretty tall. My bank account matured through the summer, and by autumn I was ready to begin flying lessons.

Dad never said much about "keeping things straight." He was a man of neither joke, nor jocundity. However, he taught us about being fathers and husbands and men. Years later we finally got him to open up about it and admit with the slightest grin that he knew exactly what Bill had been doing all morning. I believe in pivotal moments in our lives. And that rainy summer day was one. From then onward Bill did all his sleeping at home.

Chapter Nine

Everyone Needs A Mentor

During vulnerable times in our lives we are susceptible to a myriad of influences — some good, some not. A wonderful example of a mentoring character was manifested in the 1984 film, "The Karate Kid." The plot revolves around a young Daniel LaRusso, whose single mother has moved them to Reseda, CA. from New Jersey to accept a new career position. Daniel, being of dark-haired Italian descent, fails to fit in with the golden-haired surfer crowd at his new school. For a while, Daniel manages to avoid fighting. But eventually the blond bullies have their way with him; Daniel suffers several severe beatings in the hallways. During one fusillade away from school, Miyagi, an elderly gardener who happens to hold a black belt in Karate, springs to Daniel's rescue by giving the fanfaron a taste of his own medicine. Daniel and Miyagi become good friends afterward, and Miyagi teaches him not only the finer points of Karate, but also the even more important elements of life: honesty, faithfulness, devotion, and duty.

On Saturday morning, the 24th of October 1970, an impeccable autumn day, Dad drove me out to Woodrum Field. I had called the airport several days before to schedule the time for my first flying lesson. There were four businesses in the Roanoke phone directory with listings under flight schools. The first one I dialed didn't answer the phone. The second was not accepting students at the time because of a shortage of instructors. There was something chafing me about the grandiloquous presentation in the yellow pages of the third, so I didn't call that one. My choice for a flight school was simple, the only one remaining: Hillman Flying Service.

Dad parked the car along the access road, and together we hiked down the meadowy embankment to the near end of the utilitarian 'T hangar' building. A faded blue and white metal sign hung above the open doorway. "Office" was all it read. As we approached, a dapper man whom I judged to be about Dad's age, dressed in a flamboyant, red-checkered sport coat and tie beneath a shock of wavy gray hair, stepped through from the shadow and greeted us on the patio outside the office.

"Are you David?" He asked keenly while pulling a splendid pecan-colored pipe from between his white teeth.

"Yes, Sir." I said as we shook hands. "And this is my father, Clyde Sandidge."

"I'm Wes Hillman. You're here right on time."

The two men exchanged pleasantries briefly, and then Mr. Hillman turned toward me and said,

"You ready to start now?" "Yes, Sir." I replied.

"Then let's go."

He put a hand on my shoulder and guided me toward a diminutive single-engine, high-wing 1959 Cessna 150 tied down in the grass across the concrete taxi strip. Along her flank was painted, 'N7176X'. Brand new she had strutted alluringly out of the factory decked in glossy cream and burgundy with matching wheel covers. Now, after eleven years of sun and exposure, she lounged barefooted in bleached canary and faded tie-dye.

Mr. Hillman untied the ropes imprisoning the Cessna and tossed them aside. Then he helped me through the door on the left, port side of the plane - adjusting my seat as far forward as it would go. He paused suddenly with a perplexing scowl. Even with the seat locked in the full forward position, I wasn't able to see over the instrument panel, nor could I reach the pedals on the floor.

"You need to grow a little, don't you?" He chuckled. "Wait right here."

He disappeared, whistling, into the hangar behind us momentarily, and then reappeared with a broad smile while carrying two pillows. Looking over at Dad standing by the office door, I could see the big grin on his face. We put one pillow under me to sit on so I could see over the panel, and the other we stuffed behind me – so I could reach the rudder pedals. After I was snugly collocated in the Cessna, Mr. Hillman walked around to the right-hand, starboard side of the plane and climbed in with the agility of an athlete – still whistling. Thus began my first lesson.

I marveled at the numerous dials and switches on the panel in front of me – familiar with only one, the magnetic compass. I felt about as lost as an oboe player in a Rock-'n'-Roll band.

"Don't worry about all those." Mr. Hillman nodded toward the instruments as he adjusted his own seat and fastened his belt. "We'll get to 'em one at a time as we need 'em."

His hands moved expertly around the cramped cabin, snapping switches and manipulating various knobs. He flipped opened his side window, leaned out, and summarily hollered at no one in particular.

"Clear!" Then he explained: "We have to warn everybody we're about to start the engine."

"Oh." I brilliantly replied as I glanced around to see if we had attracted an audience.

He reached up and pulled a knob that resembled the 'T' handle on Dad's lawn mower – only smaller. With a grinding "Gerr…. err…err,err,err" the metal propeller began to rotate, and the little airplane shivered briefly as the engine in front of us clattered into life – settling down after about three seconds into a rhythmic "clackety, clackety" idle. The propeller became a shadowed hologram disc.

"The first instrument you need to learn about is this one." Mr. Hillman said above the drum of the motor as he touched his finger to a little glass window.

"This is the oil pressure gage. It shows us whether or not we have sufficient oil pressure to the engine for proper lubrication. If this needle doesn't rise after a few seconds, longer in the winter, shut down the engine immediately, because you have a problem. You can ruin an engine real fast if it has no oil pressure. It should come up into the green arc pretty quick." As an afterthought he said, "And don't tap on the glass."

I watched the needle rise smartly into the green arc as I wondered how I would have shut down the engine if it hadn't. I determined I would simply get out and run. Dad was still standing outside the office near the door.

Mr. Hillman then switched on two radios, quickly looked to his left and right, then inched a large black knob sticking out of the bottom of the panel in a little bit with his left hand.

"This is the throttle." He announced. "Push it in – just like the gas pedal of a car to give the engine more fuel." The puttering engine became a snarling lioness. We began moving forward slowly.

"I'll do all the taxiing, but you follow through with me on the rudder pedals." He said.

I wasn't sure what the term "follow through" meant, and he seemed to sense my bewilderment. He pointed back-and-forth with his left hand.

"Put your feet on those pedals down there and feel the movements I make with mine over here."

Doing so, I quickly determined he was steering the little Cessna around with his feet.

"See? Push left to go left. Push right to go right. How does that feel?"

"It feels spongy." I said trying to say anything containing more than one syllable. But my pillow was becoming more oblate by the second. I strained to see over the panel. Mr. Hillman laughed and said,

"Next time you'll sit on two."

We taxied a short distance to a spot just past the end of the long T hangar where he brought us to a stop. Next, he completed what he referred to as an "engine run-up." This was to insure the fidelity of various systems and instruments. Then he brought a bulky gray microphone to his lips from under the dash. In a barely audible tone while turning slightly in his seat away from me, he spoke several words into it. Immediately a man's assertive voice answered in the speaker over our heads. I didn't understand one word he said; however, Mr. Hillman replied promptly and we resumed our taxi toward the runway for takeoff.

Along the way he had me practice steering with the pedals. We weaved our way like Otis Campbell around the red brick terminal building where Dad and I had enjoyed many hours together watching airliners. On the north side of the building, laid before us like a deserted parade ground parkway, was a long black taxiway with a yellow line down the middle. It ended abruptly about three quarters of a mile ahead. My task was to use my feet to keep us on that yellow line. We passed through it many times before reaching the end.

Shortly before the turn, Mr. Hillman rotated two knobs on a radio and talked again into the microphone. I wondered why he felt like he needed to hide what he was saying as he again turned away from me as he spoke into it. A new voice answered this time. It rattled out a lengthy sentence, most of which I again failed to comprehend. But I did hear the words, "Cleared for takeoff." And I understood Mr. Hillman's reply. "Roger, 76X."

We rolled out onto the expansive asphalt runway, and Mr. Hillman slowly pushed the throttle knob all the way in until it was touching the panel. He firmly held it there. The engine roared; it was fully awake. Mr. Hillman hollered for me to follow through with him on the controls; I did. The little Cessna gained speed rapidly in the cool morning air. The controls felt more rigid as the speed increased. In only a few moments we seemed to literally jump off the ground. I watched the details of the earth beneath us grow smaller and smaller until we passed the airport boundary fence and headed out over the city ahead. The view was spectacular, but the noise of the engine, combined with the foreign dynamics of flight, effectively pulled a sensual iron curtain down over my ability to absorb much information.

I don't remember many details of that first lesson anymore except how difficult it was to carry on a conversation because of the engine noise. My senses were bombarded with new experiences which effortlessly overwhelmed my young mind. I do remember the hot mechanical smell of the airplane. At some point Mr. Hillman instructed me to look down at the ground while we were in a turn to the left.

"Do you recognize where you are?"

I looked perplexingly out my window to the ground below searching for something, anything that seemed vaguely familiar. There were farms and houses, and a railroad track curving through a dense stand of defoliated trees, but I hadn't recognized much of anything since I got out of the car.

"No, Sir." I admitted.

"We're over Bonsack." He quipped. "Don't worry about it. It won't take long to settle in. Before long you'll know the names of all the towns, lakes, rivers, and even mountains around here. We use 'em as checkpoints." He said this as he gestured with his pipe in various directions.

I believed him; but, at the same time, I wondered how anyone could ever accomplish such a feat. I did recognize one indomitable fact: Even though my thought processes had been lassoed after leaving the ground, it felt wonderful being there in the clear October sky. A jagged mountain of learning stood before me, and it had to be scaled. But to me it was like breathing – something you did without consideration. I was going to be a pilot; it was time to begin.

Back on the ground, I was introduced to Mrs. Hillman, who, behind her flower-adorned desk, served as the secretary/ receptionist. She wrote out an invoice for me, and I handed her $11.50 in exchange. Mr. Hillman advised me to schedule my lessons for every other Saturday because I wouldn't be able to solo until my sixteenth birthday – just over one year away. He said there was no need to fly every week.

Dad and I walked back up the hill to the car where I re-read the entry in my stiff new logbook. Thirty minutes had been recorded in it. In the remarks section Mr. Hillman had written: 'Control effect, ailerons, okay.' I suppose it meant I had learned something, but I wasn't quite sure what it was.

It was the beginning. Over the next four years I absorbed facts and ameliorated procedures concerning the art of flying – as well as the science of sociology. The relationships I developed around the airport would grow in many directions. There would be sound affinities and fractious animosities. Learning from each was inevitable and edifying.

I became the ineradicable fly on the wall. The "Old-Timers," who flocked together around the cast iron stove furnace in the office in the afternoons and evenings like pigeons coming to roost, dispensed their empirical knowledge like ripened apples falling to the ground. And I, as an impressionable teenage boy, ate it up ravenously. But there was more.

Hillman Flying Service radiated an irrefutable attraction that was unmistakably apparent to all who shared their lives with it. Everyone could feel it, but not many could readily identify its coalescing element. At first I couldn't either; however, as time went on, and Mr. and Mrs. Hillman tutored me in life as well as in aviation, I recognized what it was. I had been witnessing it all my life. And it had begun centuries earlier.

Chapter Ten

The Present

I returned to Roanoke in June of 2008 to sit down with Mr. and Mrs. Hillman and listen to them tell me the story of their lives together. My good friend, Larry Shelton, and I met the Hillmans at the K & W Cafeteria near Crossroads Mall in Roanoke for breakfast early on the third of June. We enjoyed an hour of fellowship with them there before following them to their home in order to talk more intimately.

Ascending the Hillmans' shaded driveway in north Roanoke County, Larry and I both felt welcomed because we knew they genuinely welcomed us. The same ardency and openhearted hospitality my grandparents shared with all who entered their home was present that morning as we relaxed on the Hillmans' lanai. The arborous panorama, garnished with a crow's irascible chastisement of some particular not to his liking, completed the ingenuous sense of goodness that surrounded us. The Bible calls it a quiet spirit. It is reflected in the faces of those who truly possess it.

Mrs. Hillman, still as lovely and gracious as when I last saw her years before, keeps very busy with her family and church activities. Mr. Hillman, now eighty-six, but still projecting that cock-a-lorum character I admired for so many years, has long since retired, but his passion and vigor for aviation has not waned. He maintains a voluminous collection of priceless photos and memorabilia spanning more than sixty wonderful years of aviation in and around Roanoke. There's nothing he enjoys more than sharing his knowledge and experience with the endless parade of visitors and admirers who enter his home. Nevertheless, as we explored a bountiful cache of aviation treasures, I felt a twinge of sadness when I mentally pictured the stark bleakness and inimical inhospitality that extravasates from Roanoke's Woodrum Field today, compared to the affability and bonhomie emanating from the photographs and newspaper clippings of decades ago.

Mr. and Mrs. Hillman shared with us many stories of their lives together. They talked of experiences during the early years of aviation in Roanoke, anecdotes about people they knew, and the triumphs and tragedies that ultimately shaped their lives together. As I switched on the tape recorder and set it before them I witnessed a virtual rewinding of archival memories through their eyes. Mr. Hillman collected his thoughts for a moment, smiled lovingly at his wife, and then began:

Chapter Eleven

A Time Before

"I can't remember a time when I wasn't crazy about aviation, even when I was a little kid. There weren't many airplanes in the air at that time. Aviation was still in its infancy. In the 30s you couldn't go out and buy plastic models like you can nowadays. You had to construct your own model planes out of balsa wood kits. You even had to cut out the wheels. But they looked like airplanes.

"In my family there were five boys and one girl. We didn't have much room to ourselves as kids. But Mom and Dad knew how I loved flying and model planes; so, whenever we'd move to a new house, they'd give me a special place just so I could hang my models from the ceiling. And I'd have shelves fixed with aviation things on them. Seemed like all I ever cared to talk about was flying. I just loved it.

"Mom and Dad used to take us kids out to the airport – such as it was - on Sundays. In those days they had Cook Field up on Lee Highway, and they had Trout Field over on the Lynchburg Turnpike – behind the Fairview Cemetery. These were simply long pastures that various folks used as landing strips. Nobody cared too much one way or the other about what they did with them. Like I said, there weren't many planes flying anyhow.

"Along about 1929, the city of Roanoke bought some land up in the north part of the county next to the old Cannaday home with the idea of establishing a permanent airfield. Clayton Lemon leased some space there and put up a hangar. So that was the beginning of the airport we know now. And eventually the city officially closed the two other airports. But there were little landing strips all over the valley at that time. Of course, there was a lot more farm land then than there is now, too.

"Well, the airport started to grow – with more airplanes coming to the valley. Ludington Airlines served the area for a while with those old three-motored Stinsons. They came out of Washington and Charlottesville. But they didn't last long, because they didn't have a mail contract with the government. American Airlines began flying into Roanoke sometime around then – as well as I can remember.

"In 1933, I finally begged Mom and Dad to bring me out to the field and let me stay all day. Even back then you didn't let ten year old kids run around all day alone in a strange place. And Mom and Dad didn't think too much of aviators, either. They kind of thought about them in the same way that most folks thought about Vaudeville actors – with their drinking, and gambling, and carrying on…. But that's not the way it really was; Hollywood just portrayed it that way.

"My Dad dropped me off under the old oak tree at the curve in the gravel road just up the hill from the two hangars on Thanksgiving Day. As I hopped out of the car Dad told me to be home in the afternoon, 'cause we were going to eat

Thanksgiving dinner about then. It was cold that day, and I had on just a worn out oversized sweater that I wrapped around me. A few people were flying, not many.

"I stood out by the fence for the longest time, well after lunch, until a man dressed in black pants, a leather jacket, and a flying helmet came to the door and hollered out across to me. He yelled, 'Come on in here kid, you look like you're about froze to death!' I didn't know I was cold. I was at the airport. And that was all I cared about.

"So I went in, and I was scared to death. I scooted in by the door and just stood – too scared to even move. There were some aviators sitting at an old kitchen table by a wood stove playing a card game and talking and so forth. I knew they were aviators 'cause they had on helmets and goggles. One of them finally looked over at me and said, 'Come on over here by the stove, boy, it's warmer.' He picked me up and set me down on a divan that was fixed to the wall near the stove. I sat there all day listening to the men talk about flying and all. Every now and then one of them would go out and carry some passengers up for a ride over the city, and I would watch them crank up and take off. I stayed out there longer than I was supposed to, and I got home way after dark. Mom and Dad didn't like it at all because they didn't know these people. They thought they were a bunch of ne'er-do-wells.

There were a lot of movies out about flying in the early 30s that glamorized aviators as drunkards, and gamblers, and daredevils. But there was no truth to it. Those men out there at the field were just as good as morally-upright people you'll ever find anywhere. Several of them even taught Sunday school and Boy Scout classes and things like that. Oh

well, on occasion they'd take a drink; I'm not going to say
they wouldn't, `cause some of 'em did. But, they never drank
while they were flying. I've seen Boots out in a cow pasture
many-a-time while we were barnstorming, and some guy
would come up to him with a jug and say, 'Have a drink.'
Boots would stick out his hand and say, 'Nope, not while
I'm flyin' this airplane, but you come back `long about dark,
after I tie her down, and I'll have one with you.'

All those guys realized the seriousness of the business
of flying, and they just didn't do the things that Hollywood
led the country into believing about aviators. They were
good people. To this day I've had one swallow of beer, two
swallows of wine, and I don't know the taste of whiskey. I've
never tasted it, because all those men out there at the airport
said, 'No! Don't even get involved with all that stuff; you
don't need it.' And they wouldn't let me. The only thing I
ever did was take up a pipe during the war.

"The only regret you might say I had was they let me
quit school before I graduated. I wouldn't listen to anybody
else, but I would listen to them – my buddies at the airport.
I guess I really didn't need any more schooling at the time
because, I knew what I was going to do with my life. I
was already doing it. I had my instructor's license before I
left school, and I was busy everyday with teaching. In fact,
some of my teachers were my students. So school wasn't
exactly a waste of time, but it did interfere with the goals I
had set for myself. But, you know, I received a wonderful
education from all the people I met at the field. They were
all older than I was, and I learned so much from them over
the years. I did stick with school as long as I could until it
started to compete with flying. And everybody knew what

I was doing; I couldn't hide anything from anyone. This one day at school – the old Lee Jr. School downtown - was a good example.

"On a Friday afternoon in Civics class my teacher, Ms. Phelps, gave all us kids an assignment to complete over the weekend. We were each supposed to pick out some official department of the city, such as the water department, garbage, police, or street departments – things like that. We were expected to learn as much about them as we could over the weekend, then come in on Monday and give an oral report on what we discovered. Well, what she didn't know was I was busy on the weekends at the airport. I didn't have my instructor's license at that time, but I did have my commercial. And I was flying people and things all over the area all weekend long. I didn't have time to learn what some high-fallutin' bureaucrat thought about garbage. I was really busy. We got started at daylight, and we stayed till it got dark – after dark sometimes. I got to thinking about that report come Monday mornin' though. But, I figured with so many kids in the class – thirty-five or six - the chances were pretty good that I wouldn't be called on.

After Ms. Phelps took the roll, she looked at me and said, 'Wesley, you'll be the first this morning to give your report.' Oh, man! I hadn't even thought about ANYTHING having to do with a report all weekend. As I stood and began to make my way to the front of the class I said to myself: "What am I gonna do?"

Ms. Phelps had not assigned anything pertaining to aviation to anybody; so I got up there and started talking about flying and aviation in Roanoke. I knew aviation, and I knew what it meant to the valley. I got up there and started talking about flying and what it was like to be a pilot. Seemed like I talked for just a few minutes or so, but the next thing I knew the bell was ringing to dismiss the class. I had stood there and talked about aviation for the whole period. I looked back surprised at Ms. Phelps, and she had a grin on her face from ear-to-ear. She never interrupted me, and I just kept on talking. I know the rest of the kids were enjoying me talking so much 'cause they didn't have to get up there to give their reports. Later on I overheard Ms. Phelps say to another teacher, 'And you could've heard a pin drop in that room.' Anyhow, I passed the whole course in that one day.

"Let's go back now to 1933. I was about eleven years old. There was this older fella' whom I looked up to as kind of a father figure; this was Boots Frantz. He and I just kind of hit it off together. I respected him like my own daddy. Since I practically lived at the airport, you could say Boots pretty much raised me and instilled in me the moral character that everybody needs to get along with others. You know, when I got to be teenager I got pretty smart-alecky; I thought I knew everything there was to know. I was a fiery character in my younger years – even as I got older. But Boots was the one who would take me by my ears and straighten me out when I needed it. Even when I was just a little boy Boots would tell me: "You can stay out here at this airport if you want to, but you're not gonna just hang around. You're gonna work!" And man, let me tell you; I worked. I was scared they'd run me off if I didn't. But I enjoyed it – every minute of it.

"Like I said before, there weren't too many airplanes in the early years. The ones they had belonged to doctors, and lawyers, and important business people. On calm sunny days, if they could break away in the afternoons, they'd drive out from town and fly a little bit. Well, those old engines, the Liberties and OX-5s and such, would throw oil and grease everywhere. You couldn't simply squirt or pour the stuff in those engines with a gun or a can. You had to remove the rocker boxes and pack the grease in. All that oil and grease would get hot and blow all over the tail and down the fuselage and everywhere. And I found out right quick that if I took a bunch of rags and wiped it all off while it was still hot those airplanes were a lot easier to keep clean and shiny. Of course, those people would be dressed up in their business clothes, and they wouldn't want to get any of that dirty stuff on them. So, as soon as they would come in, I'd walk up and start wiping down around the cockpit area so they wouldn't get oil on their clothes. They didn't know who this little kid was, and they never paid me anything. I never asked for any money. I just loved airplanes, and I wanted to be around them. So, for a long while I had all the airplanes at the field looking pretty good just by keeping the oil and grease off of them.

"After a while I got to be sort of a fixture at the airport; everybody got used to me being around cleaning their airplanes. So, frequently, they would throw me up into the front cockpit and take me with them when they came out to do a little flying. Now, they weren't instructors or commercial pilots, or anything like that, but they'd still let me handle the controls. They'd teach me what they knew and what they did in certain maneuvers and all. And that's how I learned to fly – just a little bit at a time. Later on, after a couple of years, Boots got it all together for me and taught me the other things I needed to learn before I could solo.

"He had a couple of students down at Montvale – one became an instructor, the other became a respected doctor in that area. Boots would let me fly the airplane to Montvale where he'd pick up his students for their lessons. This one particular morning we arrived early over the pasture and shot a couple of landings before his students showed up. I was doing pretty good, so he said, 'Well, you might as well go on and solo.' He got out, and I didn't say anything; I just took off and shot a few landings that morning on my own for the first time. And boy was I thrilled.

"Back then we had what they called the Department of Commerce. That was before the government came up with the CAA. And there was this inspector who would come around every month or so from Richmond to see what was happening on the local airports. Those guys in the Commerce Department were never out to crucify anybody back then, because there weren't many people in aviation, and they wanted to build it up and expand the system in the country. So they really helped us out when they could. Everybody wanted to obey the law at the time – even when there wasn't anyone around to enforce it. And we all tried to do the best we could in that area.

Well, I had soloed without a medical permit, nor did I have a student license. I never thought about it, and Boots never intentionally did anything wrong; he just didn't think about it either. So, this particular day, shortly after I soloed, the inspector showed up to check on things. We were all standing around outside the hangar, talking and carryin' on, when he asked, "Well, boys, anything exciting been going on around here?" One of the guys with us blurted out, 'Ol' Wes Hillman soloed the other day.' Now, this inspector knew very well that I didn't have a student permit, so he called Boots and me and a couple of others into the office. We all thought we were in for it then, too, but he never got excited or angry. We just talked it over, and he said for me to go on and get a permit and just not say anything about it to anyone. He knew there wasn't any malice intended, we'd just forgotten about all the rules and regulations. He was a pretty good old boy.

I got the permit after a little while – when I was old enough to get it – and Boots officially soloed me in 1939. In the mean time, I kept on flying and teaching. In 1940 I finally was old enough to take the test for the instructor's rating. When I took and passed the Department of Commerce test, that same inspector wrote out my license here in Roanoke. He also knew I'd been teaching several students down at Montvale. So when he handed me my brand new license he sort of winked at me and said, "Now you can go on back down to Montvale and solo those students you've been teaching how to fly."

"Knowledge was something we lacked back in the early days. We didn't have all these books and studies about how airplanes flew. We had to pretty much learn everything on our own. It wasn't until the late thirties that the government began extensive flight tests to learn all about what was happening when you moved the flight controls a certain way. Before that, we just went up and tried something. And if we lived through it we'd come back and tell everybody else about it; then they'd go up and try it for themselves.

If they confirmed it, then the procedure became sort of a word-of-mouth law.

"During this time anybody that held a transport license could automatically teach someone else how to fly. But after the government started to get more involved with it all they came out with new regulations that said you can't teach flying unless you held a new flight instructor's license. Well, they knew they couldn't just barge in and shut everybody down until they were able to obtain one; a law like that would have been devastating to aviation at the time. So what they did was this: They'd send the books to all the flying businesses and had the pilots study them for a while. Then, after a while, a Department of Commerce inspector would come around, sit down with everybody, and go over all the material on the test. When he felt everybody was up to speed he'd pass out an open-book test. Everybody passed, as far as I can remember. You can imagine a bunch of gruffy guys sittin' around takin' a test together – all the jokes and all. After that, the inspector would take each one of them up for a flight test. Well, they didn't know what they were doing. So the inspector would simply show `em how to do everything right then. He'd teach them the things that he wanted them to teach others the very next day. So many of the procedures we had been teaching were all wrong, and a lot of good people lost their lives because of it. But we just didn't know…. Everything seemed to get better after all of us started teaching the things the government was coming out with in the late 30s and early 40s; things improved immensely after that.

"Now, one thing I need to make very clear is this: You cannot compare modern-day aviation with flying in those early years; it was completely different back then. Forty thousand feet!? That's where angels were. Besides that, to climb to only ten thousand feet you had to take a lunch along with you. It'd take you all day to get up that high. If you took off from Roanoke and were headed somewhere across the mountains, you had to circle the valley until you had enough altitude that you could chance going across the mountains. Generally, six thousand to sixty-five hundred feet was about all you could get from those engines and airplanes. Besides, it got pretty cold up there.

"When I was an instructor for the Navy during the war, our airplanes didn't have any kind of avionic systems or electrical systems in them. We even had to hand-crank the engines. We didn't have any type of intercom other than a speaking tube that ran from the front cockpit under the floor to the back. They called it a 'gosport'. The student would attach it like he would a doctor's stethoscope. It fixed right into the helmet. That way, you, as the instructor, could talk to the student as he performed certain maneuvers. I liked it because I could holler at a student and tell him if he didn't do it right I was gonna stick the mouthpiece out into the slipstream and blow it out between his ears. They'd do it right after that. We used hand signals, too; they were very important. But, that's how we did things back then.

"Another big problem we had was carburetor ice. We knew something was causing the engines to quit so often, but we didn't know what. We had no idea about vapor condensation and ice formation inside the carburetor of an engine. We always thought it was water in the gas. They didn't even have refrigerators in those days; how were we supposed to know about ice formation? If you made it safely to the ground after your engine quit, the first thing you did was drain the jets on the bottom of the engine. Well, out would come a cup or two of water. We thought we'd just gotten hold of some bad gas. Of course, by that time all the ice that had built up in the carburetor had melted. The government finally did some studies and discovered the principal cause of the ice was the way the carburetor had to be designed in order to work properly. So, what they did was to install a system that would allow you to apply heat to the carburetor if the engine started to lose power. It would melt all the ice, and then the engine would eventually be fine - although, it would run slightly rougher for a while with the heat on. I've ridden nine airplanes to the ground with the engines out. Some of them were because of carburetor ice.

"You know, the 30s was a great era to grow up through. We had the barnstorming days – where we'd go out on Saturdays and Sundays and put on flying demonstrations. When you mention barnstorming you automatically think about the 20s, after the First World War. But barnstorming went on into the late 30s. Money was not plentiful at the time, but some of us kind of made that type of flying into a little sideline business. You had to come up with something if you wanted to eat. Long about mid- week we'd takeoff, two or three airplanes at a time, and go out to look for a suitable field - a pasture near a town. Then we'd land and go looking for the farmer that owned it to see if we could make some arrangements with him to use the field to fly out of for the coming weekend. If he agreed to the deal we'd catch a ride or walk into town to talk to various business people.

"First thing we had to do was convince an oil and gasoline distributor into providing us with those necessities for the weekends' flying. Then, most of the time, we could get a car dealership to take care of the advertising for us in the newspaper. It would say: 'So and So's flying circus was gonna be at a certain field on a certain day. Brought to you by So and So's fine cars.' So that took care of all our advertising. Sometimes we'd use Boot's old Ford truck if we weren't too far away from Roanoke. We'd fix that old thing up with those big speakers. Then we'd drive around announcing the events for the coming weekend. Old Hartman, out here on Cove road, would keep those things going for us. He'd take care of that part of the business for us. He rigged up sixteen batteries to power the sound system. I traded a guy some flying for a couple of those big ol' horns.

"One day years later, I called ol' Hartman and asked him: 'Hey, how many batteries do we need to get this set up going?' He laughed and said, "Wes Hillman, you're still living in the barnstorming days!" He said they've got new things now to power all that stuff to keep the batteries up. Guess it's some kind of generator or something nowadays. But anyhow, we'd sell ads over that thing. We'd get somebody that was a good talker to announce for us.

"Irving Sharp used to be on the radio and television here in Roanoke years ago – one of the early pioneer broadcasters. He would go with us on Sundays and announce for us over the public address system. And Irving would get to carryin' on about one thing and another. You know, he was quite a joker. He'd start telling stories and jokes, and the first thing you knew the airplanes were sittin' over here all by themselves, and everybody would be standing over there listening to him tell jokes. Boots would finally walk over and tell him to hush up and sell some tickets. Then Irving would announce to everybody that he had to stop telling jokes and get the airplanes flying or we wouldn't be able to eat that night. The soft drink, Dr. Pepper, was new in the area at that time, and old Irving could sell more bottles of cold Dr. Pepper than anybody I ever saw. He'd get all those farm folks standing around to drinking that stuff and makin' `em laugh at the same time. Now that was a sight.

"Another thing we'd do was to fix big signs on the sides of the airplanes. What it was really was advertising space. We'd get maybe fifty dollars for each sign we did. That was a lot of money back then. We'd go into a grocery store or someplace and talk to the manager. And we'd say, 'Now, Mr. So and So, where's all the eyes gonna be when that airplane is comin' in for a landing out there on that field?' And he'd say, 'Well, they're all gonna be watchin' that airplane.' And we'd say, 'That's exactly right! And your sign ought to be right there on the side of that thing where everybody can see it.' He'd say, 'Give me that pencil right now!' He'd sign the contract right then and there. So, we made a little money out of that. But I'll tell ya, the very first thing we'd try to do before we started in too far was to get the county sheriff – and get him out there.

"Of course, in those days the sheriff was as much of a politician as he was a sheriff. So we'd get him out shaking hands with folks. We'd get him up on the wing of that airplane talking to the crowd. Then we'd take him up for the first ride around the field and have him wave to the crowd down below. After that, we never did have any more problems with people parking their cars and wagons all over the place. People parked wherever they wanted to for the rest of the day. And everybody had fun and enjoyed themselves. It was a family time. It was a good time.

"Now, some of the best times we ever had were down there in Franklin County. The good people down there, 'The Old Order,' they liked to be called, they had these all-day meetings – church meetings. Revivals is what they were. And they always had dinner on the grounds at the churches. Well, sometimes our cow pasture was pretty close in to `em. So, we respected their services and didn't fly over the churches. We'd always turn away from 'em. And they appreciated that. Long about dinnertime they'd send somebody down to get us to come up there and eat with `em. And the food…! Oh, man, those people could cook! They'd pull up under those big shade trees there in wagons – mule-drawn old wagons. Down under the seat there'd be a trunk – an old humped back trunk - and they had shelves built into `em. They'd open those things up and you'd see homemade pies, and cakes, and puddings…. They'd have all kinds of dishes lined up on each side of these long tables, and you'd go down and just pile your plate full of food. You'd be walkin' over to sit down and a woman would come up and say, 'You didn't get any of my chicken; have some of my good chicken.' And she'd pile some of that tender fried chicken right on top of everything else. We ate so much we wondered if we were gonna be able to get off the ground when we got back to our airplanes. But those people down there were good, honest, hard-working Christian people who would give their word and mean it. Whatever they told you, you could count on it. They appreciated us. And let me tell you, we really appreciated them.

"There were quite a few famous aviators that came through Roanoke from time to time. I say we knew `em, but we didn't really. Flying at that time held a pretty close-knit community; it was small. Now, you may not know 'em to go up and shake hands with 'em or anything like that, pat 'em on the back and say, 'Hello Amelia, how are ya?' You may not have known them quite that well, but they'd be in the hangar or a meeting room with all the rest of the guys. You'd see `em close enough as they'd walk through. Amelia Earhart was one. I'd seen her a few times. Louise Thaden was another. Louise was actually more famous than Amelia. I mean not more famous, but at one time Louise held the top speed, altitude, and endurance records of the world. She won the women's Air Derby in 1929.

"Now, this air derby was a race that was supposed to adhere to a very strict set of manufacturers' rules for each model airplane that was entered. They took off, I believe from Los Angeles, CA, or Santa Monica, and finished in Cleveland. Well, Amelia got in the airplane and just shoved the throttle all the way in and got to Cleveland and landed. Everybody said, 'She got there first; she won the race.' But, actually, Louise won that race, because she followed the rules. She flew her airplane according to the racing committee's specifications on fuel flow and altitude and so forth. So I always knew that Louise was a better flyer than Amelia was. Louise didn't get the publicity that Amelia did because Louise married an aircraft designer, Herb, out in California. She was born in Arkansas, and she migrated to California. But Amelia was married to a famous public relations man, and that's why she got all the publicity on things.

"I first met Louise in about 1934. She'd been commissioned by the Department of Commerce to do flight checks of routes from various cities such as Washington to Nashville, and Cleveland to Atlanta. And, you see, prior to that, there was very little night flying going on, because nobody had any navigation aids or anything like that. So, the government decided to put light beacons and towers up on prominent points along the routes so pilots could fly at night. And they called the one through here 'Lighted Airway number 22', I think. It cut off here and went to Lynchburg and Richmond. There was 'Green Airway number 5', and it turned on to the northeast on toward Charlottesville and Washington. Anyway, Louise flew into Roanoke to refuel on one of these route checks. She got out of the airplane, and I gassed it up for her. When she was ready to go I gave her a crank; I hand propped the engine, and she taxied out and took off. Well, almost immediately she turned around and came back and landed. Now, me just being a kid, I was scared I'd done something wrong. I ran back out to her when she pulled up and I said, "What happened, Ms. Thaden?" She said, "Something broke on the airplane." I remember how kind she was to me. She reassured me that I didn't do anything at all. We looked all over that airplane, but we couldn't find anything. So she said, "Well, give me another crank." I reached up to crank it, and I noticed somethin' didn't look quite right on the crankshaft. I said, "Ms. Thaden, could you look at this?" She came down and looked at it, and then she just chuckled a little bit and said, "That's what it was. The spinner came off." It had actually hit the windshield, but it didn't break it. It could have – easy. If it had, things would have gone badly for her. But, it didn't.

She said, "I know what it is now, so we won't worry about it." And she went on her way.

"Louise died years ago after they had moved to High Point. Herb went into the furniture manufacturing business down there after the war. And after she died, her son, Herb Jr., who flew for Eastern Airlines for years, took one of our airplanes and scattered her ashes up here north of Roanoke. That's where she wanted to be. I believe it's somewhere between Salem and New Castle. I had a long talk with Herb before he took off. I told him, "Herb, no matter what happens up there today, you remember you've still got that airplane to control." He never forgot that. We've dropped a lot of remains, ashes like that over the years, and it's never an easy chore. Once you open that window and start pouring out of that urn, emotions run really high in the airplane. It can get dangerous. People have been known to grab the controls and freeze – or anything.

"There's another time I want to tell you about back in the barnstormin' days. We were down at another field in Vinton. We'd been flying out of this field for a few months. But the farmer let the alfalfa grow up pretty high – too high to operate out of. So that's when he told me I could move from that field up to another field on top of the hill. Well, it wasn't a good field to start with, but he kept it mowed more frequently. It was shorter than the other one, and it had a weaving mill at one end and a fence at the other. You had to come in over the fence already in the landing attitude, and you had to hit on top of that little hill. If you didn't you wouldn't have been able to stop before you ran into the mill. Well, comin' out of there we soon found out it was better to go around behind the mill and take off in the alley. So that's what we did. We just ran through there, between the buildings, and we took off from that little alley. But we had to pass under some wires then go across this fella's back yard, missing the laundry out on the line – dodging a tree on one side and the house on the other. That's another time the Lord stepped in to save me from crackin' up.

"Now, we were still in high school during this period – old Bobby Peters and me. What we'd do was, we'd get a gang of kids from school out about lunchtime, or sometimes after school – and I'd put an air show on for `em. We'd get `em out in this field over by the river - up on the hill. The river and the railroad ran down there at the bottom of the drop off – quite a ways down there to the bottom. I'd fly around doing tricks. Then I'd climb up over the river, and I'd pull her up and get it into a spin. I'd let it spin down close to the river before I'd pull it out and fly down the railroad track a ways. Well, the field where they were was way up on top of the hill, so they couldn't see me. And whoever – Bobby, or JB, would start hollerin' out, "Oh! He's crashed, he's crashed!" And all the kids would be screamin' and runnin' across the field over to the drop off to see if they could see where I'd gone down. `Bout that time I'd pop up on the other side and catch `em all right in the middle of the field. And I'd buzz right across `em all. That was the craziest thing in the world. It's a wonder we didn't hit some of those kids. I'd wheel around there and land, and all of `em would come over and let me have it, I'll tell you.

"Well, let's see. We went on like that for a few years, and then the war came along. The Navy decided to use

Roanoke as a training base for their new enlistees. We had quite a base out here at the field. I was commissioned into the Navy as a flight instructor. We were teaching basic flying skills and cross- country navigation and things. They housed the new cadets out at Roanoke College. They'd be there for the ground school and academic work, and then they would come on out to the airport for the flight training. After they got through here with that, they'd send `em down to Pensacola, Florida for advanced training. Down there they'd learn to fly bigger airplanes in formation flight. When they finished down there they'd send `em back to us for more training in instrument flying in multi- engine airplanes. One of the things we did was to teach them carrier tactics and short field take offs and landings.

We'd be out, a bunch of us, and we'd all be flying in the traffic pattern at the same time. Everybody would be cutting their engines back at different places around the field, but we'd all be aiming for the same spot on the runway to land on. You had to have your head on a constant swivel lookin' out for other airplanes. I'd tell `em, "A sore neck's better than a broken one."

"One time I had this cadet over at Timber Truss field in Salem. Now that's a really short strip over there. We were practicing short field takeoffs and landings that morning. Well, we took off and got about ten feet in the air when the engine quit. I pushed the nose over and got it back down on the ground, but we were runnin' out of runway. I got on the brakes just as hard as I could. We had brakes on that model Waco; we never had `em before. So I was pumpin' those brakes when I ground looped it to keep it from goin'

off into the Roanoke River. It swung around and put its
tail in the water.

"One time around then I had to head over to Newport
News. I was flyin' another Waco down there when I ran
into clouds and fog around Petersburg. I was flyin' over the
top of the fog bank. I thought I'd run out of it, but I didn't.
I kept goin' until I passed the no return point. I didn't have
enough gas to get back to Petersburg or anyplace. Well, you
know, we didn't have any means of navigating in clouds
or flying in clouds with those old airplanes. If you got
into clouds for very long you ran the risk of getting into a
graveyard spiral. And that was the worst thing you could do.
So I had to pull up and spin it down through the clouds.
Well, I did that. I came out of the bottom of the fog and
found an old pea patch, or something like that, and I landed
and pulled up next to the farmhouse. I got out, and the guy
that lived there walked out on the porch and told me where
Newport News was. I had to get some gas in a can to fill
the tank before I could take off though. But I finally made
it to the coast.

"So, it went like that through the duration of the war –
until the autumn of 1945. Boots had gone out to Tennessee
to start a training base for the Army at Union City. He
was out there until the war ended. Well, he came back to
Roanoke, and I was working for Paul (Piggy) Hunter. Piggy
bought the business from Boots when the war started. He
was also the manager of Hotel Roanoke at that time. He
wanted to sell the business – the flying service; but Boots
was situated a little better than I was financially. The banks
wouldn't look at me as a good risk. So Boots bought the
business back from Piggy, and I went back to work for him

– just like we had before. Things had changed around the field quite a bit since before the war, and there was a lot more flying and teaching going on at that time with the G.I. Bill and all…. It was along in there that Edith and I met for the first time. She came out to the airport with a friend of hers who wanted to introduce us. I was busy with a student right then, and I told her I didn't have time to talk. So that didn't go too well.

Boots Frantz, 1931

Wes Hillman, age 11, 1933

Woodrum Field, 1937, looking north

Woodrum Field, 1944, during the war years

The author, Greenville, Mississippi, 1958

Woodrum Field, 1970, looking northeast

Don Brown with two private pilots, 1971

The author, 1971, first solo

Hillman Flying Service and Waco F, 1973

Bernard Threet with his Ag Cat, 1972
Mississippi's Aviator of the Year

Exploring the Blue Ridge, 1984

Bill "Wild Bill" Saker, 1985

Mr. Ted Shinault, 1985

Piedmont Airlines YS-11 and Cessna N7176X

Flying cargo in 1983

Commuter airline flying, 1986

Larry Shelton and Steve Fitzgerald, 1986

Charlie Sowder, 1975

On a Christmas run to Alaska, 2004

Larry and the author, 2008

Wesley and Edith Hillman, 1997
Fifty years together

Wes Hillman, the last of the breed

Chapter Twelve

A Time Before, Part Two

It was at this point during the interview that Mrs. Hillman, who had been preparing an attractive lunch for us to enjoy, entered the conversation. She gently recalled touching scenes beginning very soon after the Second World War.

"All of my family lived in the Roanoke area. My father worked for years at the old Viscose plant beneath Mill Mountain in southeast Roanoke. You know, back then the two largest employers in town were the railroad and the Viscose operation. He did well there, but that's not where his heart was. My father loved the Lord, and he really wanted to teach the Bible. For the longest time on his lunch breaks he would go off by himself and read his Bible while sitting at a table under a tree on the grounds. Eventually, some of the men joined him and they all read together. They had prayer time. Things just seemed to grow from that.

"My father opened a small church in a tent. At first, there were just a few who came on a regular basis. But after a while more and more people joined the church. It was during the third week of these regular meetings that I accepted the Lord as my personal savior. I could feel His call on my heart, and I simply said, 'Yes, I love you.' I was baptized in a creek not far from the church. They finally built a building in the old Melrose district, and they called it the Plymouth Brethren Chapel. So, the Lord has been first in my life for practically all of my life.

"I grew up like a normal young girl, I suppose, for the times. After the war, when I was eighteen, I was working at Sears, and a friend of mine said that Bobby Peters, (Wes's friend), had someone he wanted me to meet. She said he was a pilot instructor at the airport. It was a little exciting to think about, but I wasn't sure I wanted to meet someone who was such a daredevil. After a little while I said okay. So she and I went out to the airport one afternoon on a Saturday. Bobby said Wes would meet us in front of the old terminal building. We arrived just a little bit early, and I didn't want to make it seem like we were too excited, so we waited for a few minutes until two o'clock. Then we walked over to the front of the building and sat down on a bench to wait. Bobby went in to get Wes. When they came back out Wes said hello, but he didn't have time to talk because he was soloing a student pilot at the time. So he turned around and went back through the terminal to the field. I was not impressed with that, but I did think he was very handsome and dashing. My girlfriend and I left after that. I thought I wouldn't see him again.

"After a few days he called me. Bobby had given Wes my telephone number that Bobby got from my girlfriend. We began talking on the phone on a regular basis I guess you could say. Christmas was not far away at that time, and he sent me a huge bouquet of beautiful roses and lilies. I was simply thrilled. We started courting around Christmas time.

"Back then the airport had a grassy hill right where the old terminal parking lot is now. It was more of a city park. On the weekends you'd see hundreds of people out there on blankets with picnic baskets. Children would be playing - flying kites and balloons - and dogs were running around. Those were such good times. The airport was a destination back then. It was a fun place to be. Well, at night, young couples would be out there on the hill, too. It became a favorite place to go courting and dating – sometimes very late into the night. But I won't talk very much about that.

"Wes and I dated for two years. Sometimes, when I was down in Franklin County with my family or friends we had there, Wes would fly over in his airplane and do some stunts for us. My father didn't like it one little bit, he thought Wes was a showoff. But, secretly, I was so excited. All my girlfriends would be so jealous that I had such a daring, brave boyfriend who could fly airplanes like that.

"On occasion, Wes would attend my father's church on Sunday mornings, but not too often, because he was always busy on the weekends. That should have told me something right there, but I was so much in love – starry-eyed, you know…. When he did attend, my father usually had something to say about pride and haughtiness. But Wes wasn't too awfully boastful. He was just cocky – like a Banty Rooster. I never told him that; he was though. And he had such a temper. You didn't want to be around him when he got mad.

"Every so often Wes would put me in his open cockpit airplane; I'd have my helmet and goggles on, you know. He'd fly us over to Montvale – to the little grass strip they had by the highway. We'd walk across the road to Buford's

106

café to get some of their homemade pie. They had the best pies and cakes there. It was such a lovely valley at the time. That was before they built all those oil tanks on the airstrip. There's a hangar over there that is used by a trucking company, I believe. It's still there.

"We finally were married on April 8, 1947 at the Melrose Chapel. Wes was working for Boots Frantz at the time, and Boots was good to us, but Wes was a good instructor who brought in quite a bit of business for him. Everybody knew Wes around the Roanoke area – and around this part of the country too. We moved into a house in the Rugby area off Orange Ave. after we were married. Wes's mother lived with us for a while, and I didn't like that. She and I never got along very well. But she remarried, after oh, many months, and she moved out. So it was okay then.

"After a while, Melinda, our daughter came along. She was born on March 8, 1948. And we were so proud of her. But, Wes was gone all the time - it seemed like. He was almost never around on the weekends. I spent a lot of time alone with Melinda and several other wives and young mothers.

"In 1951, Wes came home one evening and announced that he was going to buy the business from Boots. Boots had been talking about retiring from full-time flying about then. He had done very well for himself through the years, and he wanted to do some other things. Well, I didn't like it one bit. I thought Wes was gone enough already as it was. I knew if he owned the business I'd never see him. He was still in love with flying…. As a matter of fact, I thought at that time that he loved flying more than he loved me. So I simply told him that if he bought the business I would take

Melinda and leave him. You know what he said? He said, 'Don't let the door slam on your way out.' That's what he said. And he meant it, too. We had a terrible time around our home for a while. It was not pleasant at all.

"Wes signed the papers at the bank on May 15, 1951. So, he owned the business. And, of course, he changed the name to 'Hillman Flying Service.' He was so excited, but I hated it. He tried for several days to get me to come out there and answer the phone for him. Finally I agreed to come out for, I think, two or three days. I realized I was his wife, and I knew how much it meant to him. So, I bundled Melinda up and we drove out that first morning. I, of course, wasn't in a very good mood. I was going to show him that I was right. But you know, after the second day, I found myself having a wonderful time. We were busy and out of the house. I could watch Melinda, and everybody loved her. She was having so much fun. So by the end of the week I don't think you could have driven me away from the airport. I absolutely fell in love with our business. It was no longer Wes's business. It was OUR business. The Lord always works in your life for good, and it took me a while to remember that. Even without a vacation away from flying for more than thirty years, I wouldn't trade one single day of any of those years for all the money in the world.

⬥⬥⬥⬥

"Yeah, it was rough going for a little while around the house, but I knew I had to get her out to answer the phone for me because I couldn't afford a secretary. Well anyway, it didn't take long for her to absolutely fall in love with the place. I couldn't get her to leave at night. You know, many a time we'd have picnic lunches in the office for everybody. The ladies would bring out homemade dishes and things. We would even have homemade ice cream. I bought one of those big old clackety movie projectors at the flea market one Saturday morning. And I'd go into town to the armory or to the Naval reserve center to pick up some films that they had, and we'd all sit out on the patio in the evenings – sometimes until eleven or twelve o'clock watchin' those old movies.

"Back then Piedmont Airlines had several crews that would lay over for a couple of hours here in Roanoke before they'd head on to someplace. We'd see the pilots and the stewardesses walking around just looking at airplanes. We got to know several of them. They'd come in for coffee and cookies. One time while we were having homemade ice cream two pilots came by and we gave them some. This one fella was from New York. He said, "You know, I've always heard about homemade ice cream, but this is the first time I've ever tasted it." I think that day we had peach.

"So anyway, we always tried to make our business more than just a business, it was more like home. When Melinda got older she realized those propellers were very dangerous. So when some of the students would bring their families out with them while they took a lesson Melinda would take the kids around to the other side of the office to her sand box, or play volleyball, and they'd play out there. So, everybody got involved with something. In the summertime Melinda washed those airplanes just like I used to do. It's funny, after she'd go back to school in the fall everybody would say, 'I guess Melinda's back in school; all the planes are dirty again.'

"A whole lot of times a storm would come up in the afternoons. The wind would be blowing, and it'd get dark and start raining. Sometimes we'd make it back to the field before the rain and wind, and sometimes we wouldn't. We'd come around to land on the old runway two-seven, and we'd see Edith and Melinda, their hair blowin' all over, standing out next to the runway there to catch ahold of the wing struts so we wouldn't get blown over while we taxied to the hangar. They'd cling to that thing like it was their savior.

"One time the wind did get under the tail as we were taxiing a J-3 off the runway. It lifted the tail up so the prop hit the ground and broke up. It splintered that old wooden propeller into a hundred pieces. I had that prop mounted on the wall of the office for years after that - just to show the students what could happen. We lost a prop, but we never lost an airplane.

"Along about 1954, we had a young fella come out to learn to fly with us. This was Don Brown. He'd just gotten out of the Army and he wanted to use his G.I. benefits to take flying lessons. Don was about the quietest and shyest guy you'd ever meet. But he was a natural-born pilot — I'll tell you that. I took him all the way through — up to his commercial and instrument ratings. After that, I asked him if he'd be interested in becoming an instructor. He thought about it for about two seconds, and then he jumped on it. Well, we got him his instructor's license, and I hired him to go to work for us.

Don was a gentle soul who never had a bad word to say about anybody. Since I was pretty busy with most of the office work as well as teaching, I couldn't take the time to ride with the students anymore on their dual cross-country flights. So we gave all that to Don. Over the years he got to know everybody over in Lynchburg and Danville and Raleigh-Durham. Those are the places we'd send the students for their cross-country training. Don stayed with us for about thirty years before he retired.

"We had a few students go through who became instructors at one time or another. One other young man we really liked was a fella by the name of Bob Reed. Bob also started lessons in the mid-fifties I believe. Bob went through with Don for his private license, and then I think I remember he joined the Marines after that. So he was gone for several years. But he came back after a while to finish up with his instructor's license, and we took him on with us. He worked over at ITT for years and instructed for us on the weekends. Of course, Boots was around too to help out if we got too many students on the books. He just didn't fly all the time.

"You know, out of all the silly things I've done with flying over the years, there was only one time that I came close to meetin' my Waterloo. I was up early this one morning with old Warren Gilbert, who was a photographer around Roanoke for years and years; everybody knew Warren. He needed to take pictures of the area where Interstate Highways 64 and 81 were gonna come together, and he needed that early light. Now, I had just bought this brand new 1967 Cessna 172 – blue and white. That was 'November 2845 Lima.' That was the tail number on it. Anyway, we were up there around the Waynesboro airport this morning toolin' around there. I had the power back with about ten degrees of flaps down – just going around in a wide circle so Warren could shoot out the open window like he needed to. The sun hadn't been up very long at that time. We came around to the south, and right there in the windshield was another 172, same model, same year, same color. We were on a collision course. He was on a base leg to the Waynesboro airport - only a mile or so from us. It was so early I never thought anybody would be up at that time around there. I had just a split second to whip the controls over to bank out of the way, and he passed off our right side – just feet away; we heard him go past us. Ol' Warren turned white as a sheet, and I'm pretty sure he could have said the same about me.

"Speaking of Warren, we could have all been millionaires. The state and local governments used our airplanes all the time for photography missions. Back in the 50s and 60s, we knew where Interstate 581 was gonna be. We knew where Interstate 81 was gonna be – long before anybody else knew. We knew exactly where the Smith Mountain Dam was gonna be, and we knew what was gonna be under water after it was completed. You know, we could've bought up all that farm land around these places for next to nothin' and then just sat on it until the government needed to get it. They'd have paid us so much more than what we would have paid. We could have all retired long ago. But it seems like we were born under a different set of rules back then. We just didn't have the heart to do that sort of thing, because we felt like we would have been taking advantage of good people who didn't have access to what we knew at the time. Boots and I have talked about those things many a time, and we both feel the same way about it. We simply couldn't do that sort of thing. But, you know?

Everything turned out all right. I've been blessed so much in my life. The Lord has been so good to all of us.

"One last thing I wanted to say is that I was proud of my train collection. You know, Roanoke has always been a railroad town; that's why it's even here – the railroad – Norfolk and Western. Over the years, going to the flea markets around here on Saturdays, I collected over two-hundred engines and all types of cars and things. Up over the office in the attic up there, I put up three track layouts across the entire attic. I had three different scales of trains. It didn't take long for word to get around about Wes's model trains, and I got to be pretty famous because of it. Pilots would come in from all over the region. They'd fly their bosses in for a day of business downtown, and while they were waiting for them to come back they'd stop in here to pass the time of day and talk. Some of `em would kind of shuffle and hint around about the trains, and I'd finally say, 'You wanna go up and play with my engines?' They'd jump up and say, 'Yeah!' I'd tell `em to go on up and have some fun, but just don't run the engines off the table. Those guys would stay up there all day long playin' with those trains.

"So, we had a lot of fun all through the years. We got to know so many people – thousands of people. And the cards and letters we would get…. That's what life is about. It's not about making money. It's about people, and how you treat them, and the love of friends and family. Everybody says all the time, 'Wes, Edith was the backbone and heart of the business.' And they're right. She kept things connected with civility out there. Oh well, you know, a bunch of men sittin' around; things can get pretty rough. But Edith brought a calming effect to the business.

"It's just like diagnosing a problem with an engine. You dig and dig until you trace it all the way back to a specific point. Well, the success, not just in dollars, but the overall wholesomeness in a person's life can be traced back to one thing: a personal connection with the Lord. That's the secret of success. That's what I've learned over all these years of learning. Edith never let the business interfere with her devotion to the Lord. He always came first in her life, and I knew it. Everybody knew it; just not everybody would admit it. Use to bother me at times - before I got saved myself. Her church work and attendance always came first. We'd be so busy out there on Sundays, but you'd never see Edith until the afternoon when church was over. I know now that the Lord was blessing this business all along because of her. And the Bible says that in black and white. But I didn't read it until years later. That's why we were so successful over the years - not because of what I did or didn't do, or anything. It was God's blessings all the time. He is what made our business a place that everyone wanted to be a part of. He was welcomed there, and His presence touched everyone's soul – whether they realized it or not."

Chapter Thirteen

Beer and Gravity Don't Mix

Isaac Newton was a brilliant man. Among other things, he opened the eyes of the world to the mysterious geophysical law of gravity. Most of us are aware of his hypothesis concerning the physical properties of gravity. Even if we never learned to explain it we all learned about gravity as children. Additionally, from the time we were about three months old, we learned to equate the law of gravity with the word "no." And as we lolled about pithlessly in our polypropylene high chairs, clad immodestly in wrap-around maxipads contemplating the effect of gravity on a bowl of strained peas, we quickly learned Mommy and Daddy both gave much credence to the law of gravity. However, for some of us, the equation: gravity + no x 2 = lack of damaging consequences, is not truly assimilated until much later in life.

A wonderful aspect of Hillman Flying Service on Saturdays was the opportunity to meet so many interesting people. Everybody came out on Saturdays – especially pleasant ones. If the schedule was full, and no planes or instructors were available, you merely hung around – trying not to get in the way of business. Mrs. Hillman was always gracious and friendly, and Mr. Hillman was usually ebullient about one thing or another. He was always full of energy. Most of the time I arrived early for my lessons so I could marvel at all of the photos and memorabilia they had affixed to the walls of the office.

It was evident that history abounded there. Photographs of aviators from way back in the twenties and thirties whispered from every aperture that would accommodate one. On this particular Saturday in mid- November, I noticed a broken wooden propeller mounted on the wall above two cream-colored leather chairs, and I made a mental note to ask Mr. Hillman what the story behind it was. Displayed beneath it was a photograph which captured my attention and held me transfixed for a moment. It was a close up shot of a very attractive woman, perhaps thirty years of age with short dark hair, standing unpretentiously with her delicate hand resting on the fuselage of a biplane. They were positioned in front of a white hangar. She wore a heavy, fur-collared jumpsuit, and she possessed the softest eyes I think I had ever seen in a photograph. The photo was marked with the date '1938'. She had autographed it, but I couldn't make out the signature. I asked Mrs. Hillman who she was, and she told me she was a woman by the name of Louise Thaden - a long-time friend of theirs. I had no idea who Louise Thaden was, but I decided to research her in my schools' library.

As I mentally traced her delicate features, a fleeting shadow of yearnful longing passed briefly through me, and I momentarily felt very out of place – as though I had been born at the wrong time. Something inside of me pined for something else – something that I felt I was missing in my life; something I should know, or have, but didn't....

Mr. Hillman walked over, snapping me out of my mental time warp, and informed me we would be going up in a few minutes just as soon as his other instructor, Don Brown, returned with his student. In about five minutes they taxied in and shut down. We met them about half way to the plane, and then Mr. Hillman and Mr. Brown began a muted discussion about something pertaining to the airplane. So, I said hello to the other student, appearing to be only two or three years older than myself.

"Hi, I'm Dave." I said shyly.

"I'm Steve. Steve Fitzgerald." He said to me in a deeply rooted Appalachian brogue that artfully accented both syllables in the name Steve – "stay," and "eve." "Stayeve."

I asked him if he had been flying for long, and he told me he was preparing for his Private Pilot's flight test. He said Mr. Brown wanted to fly with him for three or four more hours before he turned him over to Mr. Hillman for the test. I was about to depart on my third lesson, so I knew Steve had logged many more hours than I had. And I thought I could glean from him some useful stratagems. So moving quickly I asked him,

"Are you leaving right away after you're done in the office?"

"No, I thought I'd hang around a while. I've got a couple of friends with me today; they're around here someplace. They might be down there at Bill Saker's hangar." He pointed down the long row of blue and tan hangars. "Bill's hangar is the last one down there."

So I said,

"If ya'll can wait till I get back I'd like to talk to you." Steve answered,

"Okay. Yeah, I'll be here for a while; it's a good day to be out." "Yes, it is." I agreed.

Mr. Hillman and I climbed into 76X and blundered out to the practice area over Cave Spring – with me all the while trying to hold a steady airspeed in the climb. And, all the while receiving a trumpeting ear full from Mr. Hillman about what a lousy job I was doing.

"Use that rudder!" He admonished me with a well-placed elbow to my right arm.

That day, Mr. Hillman attempted to teach me how to make turns, both left and right, while climbing and descending, as well as flying level. I never realized how difficult it would be to think in three dimensions - although my mother would have testified under oath, judging from the amassed pile of dirty clothes in my bedroom, that I was constantly thinking in three dimensions. There were so many factors to resolve at one time: throttle, carburetor heat, ailerons, rudder, "My pillows are truncating," elevators, engine temperature, airspeed, altitude, Laura's party…. I always believed Mr. Hillman was among the smartest men I ever had anything to do with. He knew the exact moment when my mind strayed from what I should have been thinking about. With his left arm draped across the back of my seat he'd reach up and pound the dash with his right hand.

"Get your mind on what you're doin', David!" He would bark. The man was clairvoyant.

After a few minutes I started to relax and get the hang of what I was doing, and we finished the lesson with me feeling like I had done a fairly good job overall. Mr. Hillman seemed to be pleased at my progress, and he laughed and joked on the way back to the field. He asked me,

"Do you know where you are?"

I looked down, and to my surprised joy I recognized the intersection of Route 419 and Apperson Drive. The Roanoke River flowed north to south just west of the intersection.

"Yay!" I said silently.

"Yes sir." I announced with confidence. "I recognize these roads down here."

"Good!" He praised. "You're learning."

Mr. Hillman endorsed my logbook for the day's lesson, and I hopped on my bicycle with a smile across my face and peddled down the taxiway to search for Steve and his friends. I found them inside Bill Saker's hangar playing some sort of dice game. They had constructed a small table against the hangar wall, and the dice were logging more airtime than anyone else that Saturday.

"Hey, come on in here. You wanna play craps?" I heard from an ariose voice as I parked my bike outside the open hangar doors.

I walked into the darkened cavern around some airplanes and located the herald that had invited me in.

"Aw, you're just a young squirt, aren't cha? I wish I was that skinny."

That was my first introduction to Bill Saker. Many people around Roanoke knew him more intimately as "Wild Bill" Saker. It would be a couple of years before I got the story behind that appellation. Bill was a character unlike any I had ever met. At the time, I judged him to be about fifty years old with white wavy hair, movie star eyes, a smooth complexion, and a trim, white mustache. He was somewhat portly, and I guessed he didn't miss many meals. He wasn't what I would have said to be overweight – just solidly round. He wore a distinctive woolen flat cap, and he carried it like a man who had seen very few failures and disappointments in his lifetime. His smile was unpretentious. Mr. Saker, jolly in his Twin Comanche airplane, had become a local legend in the Roanoke valley as well as in Atlantic City, New Jersey. I never called him "Sir" though. I just called him "Bill."

I didn't say anything as I walked in. Steve said hello again, and he introduced me to his friends. Charlie Sowder was tall and thin. To me he appeared to be about twenty-five years old. He had thick black hair and a black mustache. He looked almost exactly like the rum icon, Captain Morgan. Charlie shook my hand hurriedly, and his nervous eyes gave me a cursory glance. Then he quickly asked me if I had any money on me. I immediately assumed his prowess at the gaming tables was lacking in finesse, which explained Mr. Saker's certitude.

Larry Shelton was a different sort altogether. Larry was very tall - too tall for his weight - and lanky. He easily reached six feet, eight inches. He didn't walk, he lumbered. Watching him lurch along gave one the impression of a malleable pine tree attempting the Jitterbug in a Walt Disney animation. Larry was older; I would have said thirty years of age at the time. But he gave me the impression of a much younger man. The softness of his eyes broadcasted a countenance that radiated a child's innocence. Larry was a gentle soul who needed guardianship, and I knew from the start that he and I would be friends.

Steve said he had to get back home soon because his father had ordered him to clean the alley behind their house that afternoon. Charlie wanted to stay a while; he was down too much money. So, Larry offered to put my bike in the trunk of his car and drive me home after he took Steve to his house on Maple Avenue. I called Dad to ask him about the arrangement. He said he wanted me home by suppertime. Cleared to go, we loaded up and took off for old southwest Roanoke. During the drive I got acquainted with the two of them a little more.

Steve and Larry had met several years before at Larry's father's garage business – Shelton Motors – over in Salem. Mr. Fitzgerald and Mr. Shelton had been friends since 1943. In the effective years of their friendship their sons had become acquainted. Although many years his junior, Steve befriended Larry, and he quickly became his modern- day pundit. They were both captivated by airplanes and amateur radio – among other things. Larry told me that Charlie had worked for his Dad off and on for the past six years. He was a good mechanic, but sometimes he wouldn't show up for work. He said with a hearty laugh,

"Charlie Sowder is interested in two things: Fast cars and faster women, and not necessarily in that order."

He also said all three of them hung out together at the garage quite a bit. I was able to ask Steve several questions about learning to fly with Mr. Hillman during the ride. His most congruous advice during the course of the conversation was the exhortation for me to invest in a set of very dense earplugs. I asked him if it was because of the engine noise, and he replied,

"No. It's because of all the yelling and screaming Mr. Hillman does in your ear."

Having already experienced Mr. Hillman's colloquialistic emendations first hand, I concurred.

We took a short detour on the way to Steve's home for a quick bite to eat. Because he lived so close to downtown, he suggested we stop in at the Texas Tavern on Church Avenue for hot dogs and a bowl of chili. The tiny brick restaurant, which was little more than an appurtenance attached to a large multi-story building, emanated an innocent harlequin personality glistening with a jellied appearance in glossy white paint. Its cornices were high-lighted in high-gloss firehouse red. In fact, at first glance, I imagined a child's play house, or a Las Vegas wedding chapel. It was the perfect example of a hole-in-the-wall business. Seating a mere ten people at a time on red vinyl bar stools, it was Steve's favorite hangout because it was groovy for teenagers to be seen there. As we sat at the stainless steel counter enjoying the steaming hot chili, Larry summed the establishment's charm succinctly.

"Sure is pretty, isn't it?" He said.

I nodded in agreement. It was then that Steve made us a generous offer.

"If you guys will help me clean up the alley, I'll pay for lunch." I thought for a moment or two, and, not having a pressing need to return home before the evening, I accepted. Larry also agreed. We finished our hot dogs and headed over to Steve's house.

Mr. and Mrs. Fitzgerald lived at the top of the hill on Maple Avenue just up from Walnut Avenue. Theirs was an older, picturesque neighborhood. All of the homes were two-story brick structures with relaxing front porches. They had seen their glory during the heady days of the 1920s. Cracked and root-leavened sidewalks paralleled the street on both sides beneath gnarled maple trees. Black wrought iron fences guarded most of the front yards. As we ascended the wide concrete lane my mind clearly pictured what the neighborhood had looked like decades before. I could almost see Jackie Gleason and Glynis Johns walking arm-in-arm, adorned in derby and bonnet, pushing a baby carriage while smiling politely to all the neighbors – like they did in the movie, *Papa's Delicate Condition.* And for a fleeting moment I felt a sense of déjà vu. I belonged in a setting like that. But at the same time, it was strange to me.

We walked up the step onto the front porch where Mr. Fitzgerald was reading his newspaper. Steve introduced me to his father. He wore khaki pants and a dark blue cardigan sweater. He vaunted a thick, wavy crop of silver hair, and he brandished a starchy character replete with a seamless military bearing as he gave me a dubious nod. Steve informed me that his father had been an engineer for the Norfolk and Western Railroad since 1942. I was sufficiently impressed, and that seemed to satisfy Mr. Fitzgerald's self-regard. He returned to his paper - smiling with admirable confidence.

Inside, Steve's mother was busy in the large sunny kitchen that smelled of wonderful Italian cooking. I said hello to her, and she was very cordial and polite in greeting me. Mrs. Fitzgerald was an attractive woman – for a mother that is. She was still thin, and she wore her hair in somewhat of a beehive hairdo – like most of the women did. She did not wear glasses. When she asked if we were going to stay for supper, Steve said we might.

And as she wiped her hands on her apron she seemed genuinely pleased at the prospect of unexpected company at dinnertime.

"I always fix more than we can eat. You all are more than welcome to stay and eat with us."

After calling Dad again to ask for his permission to stay, I told her that she was very gracious to invite us. Larry brashly asked her what they were having for supper. Completely unfazed, she looked at him and winked.

"We're having your favorite, Larry. Squash casserole." They all laughed; I guessed it was an inside joke.

The three of us made our way out the back door across the yard then through the rusty gate to the alley running along behind all the houses. There were four battered metal trashcans sitting beside the wooden fence. Next to them stood two veteran yard rakes. A varied assortment of dross and bric-a-brac had been discarded around the alley; all of it was blanketed with newly-fallen maple leaves. I looked down the alley toward Walnut Avenue – about one-hundred or so yards away. It was a fairly steep slope all the way down to the street. A moth-eaten, broken down International flatbed truck sat abandoned on one side of the narrow lane. Steve wasted no time in doling out our tasks for the afternoon.

"Why don't you guys grab those rakes and pile all this trash up over here next to the fence. I'll go in and get some garbage bags to put it in." He chided Larry with a jocose warning as he pointed across the alley.

"Hey, Too Tall! Watch out for snakes in those leaves over there." Larry did a double take on the geography in question. Evidently, he was very afraid of snakes.

Steve disappeared through the gate, and Larry and I went to work. I figured we wouldn't see much of Steve until the fun was about over. And I also wondered - just for a moment – if Steve, by any chance, had ever met my brother…. I sighed a big sigh and started raking. Larry looked at me with entreatment and asked with woeful seriousness,

"Dave, you don't think Mrs. Fitzgerald is really fixin' squash, do you?"

Larry and I raked and picked up and otherwise toiled for about twenty minutes before Steve returned with the bags. We filled eight large plastic bags to overflowing. Larry asked Steve what he wanted him to do with an old tire he found lying over on the opposite side of the alley by a doddered shed. Steve told him to pick it up and lean it against the trashcans so the garbage men could throw it in their truck when they came on Tuesday. Larry did so. In a little while, Steve announced that we had cleaned well enough to pass his father's inspection. So, with that, we wiped our hands and escaped to Steve's room where we could fool around with his HAM radio equipment – practicing our Morse Code until suppertime.

Mealtime around the Fitzgerald household resembled more of a military exercise than it did a social event. Mr. Fitzgerald barked orders about where we were to sit, what utensils were needed for specific dishes, and how napkins were to be placed on one's lap. Mrs. Fitzgerald dished her husband's plate first, and then the rest of us were free to help ourselves as desired. She was very talkative and mellifluous at the table. He was quiet and amorphous while downing his supper. As we dined I asked Mr. Fitzgerald about his job as an engineer. He told us that he had been hired as a brakeman in 1942, when he was seventeen. He wanted to join the service after his eighteenth birthday; however, railroad employees were considered essential workers during the war, and they would not allow him to leave his job to join the Army. I had always harbored a yearning fascination for trains, and I expressed that sentiment to him.

"It's a good job – harder than most people think. It takes years to learn to operate a long and heavy consist up and down steep grades without pulling the train in two. I'm hoping Steve will give up this silly notion of flying and join the railroad when he gets out of school."

I glanced at Steve; he was wordless. Most assuredly, there was a little father-and-son friction going on behind the scenes.

We were about finished with dinner when we heard the twanged wrawl of Johnny Cash and June Carter singing their hit tune, *Jackson*, echoing from the street. Then there was a spirited knock at the front door. Immediately, the door flew open, and Charlie swaggered in and bellowed with a grin.

"Am I late?" Steve said,

"Come on in, Charlie, we're about through."

Mrs. Fitzgerald stood and welcomed him with a big hug, and then she went to the kitchen to retrieve another place setting. Charlie pulled a chair up to the table near Mr. Fitzgerald and told him he'd been out to see Bill Saker all afternoon. Mr. Fitzgerald tossed his head backward, laughed out loud and asked him if he'd won or lost. Charlie replied while shaking his head,

"Well, let's just say Bill's gonna have a right good time tonight, I'll tell ya that!"

Mr. Fitzgerald told him the railroad was still hiring brakemen, and he implored Charlie to come down to the yard on Monday. Charlie politely declined the offer. He said he was making too much money in Franklin County to quit.

"Charlie, they're gonna catch you one of these days; then where will you be?" Mr. Fitzgerald said ominously.

"They ain't never gonna catch me, Bob. I got the fastest car south of Poag's Mill." He retorted.

Charlie smiled, thanked Mrs. Fitzgerald for the plate, and began dishing his supper. Steve leaned over and whispered in my ear,

"Moonshine."

We relaxed around the table for a while as Charlie lamented the days' losses to Bill's underhandedness at the crap table. All the while, Mr. Fitzgerald admonished him to give up that crazy running. Mrs. Fitzgerald smiled and nodded politely at each of us in turn. Steve didn't say much. Larry kept trying to absentmindedly change the subject. And all I could think of was how much my life had begun to change in only six hours….

After supper, Steve, Charlie, Larry and I excused ourselves and went out back to the alley. Darkness had come early on that crisp November evening, and the air offered a slight chill, just enough to make us want to run – even without having any particular destination. We exuded restless energy; Larry, too. We threw rocks down the hill for a while – attempting to blast some pretend enemy bunker. Then Steve suggested we walk down to Garland's Drugstore for cherry Cokes and ice cream sandwiches. Larry agreed, saying that was a good idea. It was about then when Charlie found the tire Larry had set against the trashcans earlier in the day.

"Hey, I know. Let's roll this old tire down the alley to see how far it'll go." He suggested.

"Naw, that's no fun. It'll just fall over some place down there. Besides, it might hit something and break it." Steve replied.

"There ain't nothin' down there TO break – 'cept some trash cans." Charlie countered.

Larry warned, "We'd better not do that, Charlie. It could go pretty far."

"I betcha I can make it at least half way down to Walnut." Charlie wagered.

He looked at me. I threw my hands up and said not a word. Steve thought for just a second, and then he forthrightly proclaimed:

"You're crazy, Charlie! You'll never get it to go that far."

That's all he needed. Charlie defiantly picked up the tire and cocked it firmly in the middle of the alley. He hesitated for a moment, aligning the tire with some make-believe target. Then he gave it a very gentle push toward glory. None of us uttered a sound; we simply watched it roll past the old truck and quietly disappear into the darkness of the night.

In every horror movie I ever sat through, the entire audience knew what was about to happen to the hapless victims in every scary climactic scene. Your skin crawls as you cling to the edge of your seat shouting, "NO! Don't go in there!", while maudlin blondes stumble blindly toward their doom. Most consequences are predictably axiomatic.

The four of us closed rank in the middle of the alley to listen for any sound of a crash. After several tense moments we had heard nothing. About then I noticed for the first time, strangely enough, that down on the other side of Walnut Avenue lay something other than a vacant lot. In fact, there were several businesses down there. Their front doors were neatly juxtaposed along the front of a small, ram-shackled shopping center. The business capturing my immediate attention at the moment was a rowdy bar named George's Rendezvous.

George's place was a rather notorious hangout for a rough and ready Saturday night Country and Western crowd. I had seen the local news channels reporting on shootings and stabbings near George's over the past year. It aired an ominous desultory atmosphere indicative of its clientele. It was the type of establishment none of us, except maybe Charlie, had any business walking in to. And this Saturday night promised no exception to that warning. The place was profuse with misfiring, testosterone-clogged, drunken synapses. I surveyed the scene at the bottom of the hill and noted there were no cars parked in the scanty lot directly between us and the recessed doorway of George's. The door was in perfect alignment with the center of the alley. I remember thinking to myself,

"No. It's virtually impossible."

Several more breathless moments went by. Steve said, "Ya'll hear anything?"

I was about to answer in the negative when, to our surprise, we each saw the tire roll soundlessly into the narrow cast of a streetlight standing about mid way down the alley. It was as if Charlie had put the thing on a rail. The tire was rolling straight- as-an-arrow down the middle of the alley toward Walnut Avenue. Quick as a wink, it disappeared again in the darkness past the streetlight. Charlie struck a triumphant pose and flashed a huge white Captain Morgan grin. Steve arched his brow and said everything that needed to be said with one beautifully simple and eloquent word,

"Charlie?"

Larry looked like a deer caught in the headlights. I'm not sure what I looked like, but I had a bad feeling about it all.

We immediately became concerned about the traffic on Walnut Avenue. It was early on Saturday night, and there were many people out and about. I suddenly felt ill. We were all beginning to see that a disaster of our own doing could be in the making, but it was too late. Whatever was going to happen was out of our control. We stood helpless–but–hopeful for several more seconds. I would have given anything to hear a crash at the bottom of that alley.

We watched a car pass swiftly at the bottom going west. Next, we saw one pass going east. Then to our inevitable horror, the out-of-control missile barreled under the streetlight at the bottom of the hill – still true in its trajectory. In about one second, the black orb streaked across Walnut Avenue, hit the curb on the other side, and proceeded to launch pell-mell into the night sky. In shock, we witnessed the rubber dreadnaught bounce four times across the parking lot of George's Rendezvous and disappear squarely into the recessed entryway of the bar. We couldn't move. All four of us were frozen in place with wide-eyed disbelief – our mouths flatteringly agape…. It took about two seconds for the sound of the crash to reach us. When it did, it echoed throughout the neighborhood like the crack of a canon on the fourth of July. BOOM! Boom! What we witnessed next was truly a sight to remember.

A few years before that night, I happened upon an expansive anthill while living in Houston. I had never seen one quite so large. The soil material the ants had used resembled the bird shot that a hunter might shoot to stop small game without destroying the looks of the animal. In the heat of the day there were no ants about on the exterior of the mound. Curious, I put my foot down on top of the mound firmly. I then pulled it back. For several seconds I saw no evidence of life below the surface. The mound remained quiet and seemingly abandoned. However, after a moment or two I must have witnessed a million maddened ants racing out of that mound – each one seeking vengeance on whatever was attacking their home.

In about fifteen seconds there were fifty screaming, cussing, drunken patrons piling out of that bar looking for blood. You could see them shaking their fists and arms, and storming about - enraged as they looked up the alley to where we were hiding. Many of them were women. Several of the herd headed for their cars - I assumed to race up the alley in search of the pranksters. Charlie was wild. He stood in the cloaking darkness of the alley and let out a true Rebel Yell.

"YeeeeeeeHaaaaaaah!" Then he cupped his hands and hollered down the alley as loudly as he could,

"YOU STUPID REDNECKS!!"

I looked at Steve; he was as white as a ghost. Larry had long since vanished. Just as the first car skidded rakishly into the alley and began squealing up the hill, the three of us took off through the gate and sought refuge in the Fitzgerald's basement beneath the stairs. For about thirty minutes we heard horns honking, sirens blaring, bottles breaking, and people shouting and cursing. We never did see Larry anymore that night. Steve had told me earlier that

Larry was from West Virginia, and I assumed that's where he was headed.

We hid in the darkness – scared to death for about an hour without making a sound. We expected to hear the doorbell ring at any moment – the police searching for us. Mr. and Mrs. Fitzgerald, calmly watching an episode of Mannix, seemed to think all the commotion was indicative of a normal Saturday night around the neighborhood. They never asked us what we had been doing; neither would Steve volunteer the information. After a while though, things calmed down. But we didn't go back into the alley that night. Later, I insisted Charlie drive me home, and I wondered if I would ever see Too Tall again.

Chapter Fourteen

Bad Landing Recoveries

"Travel is fatal to prejudice, bigotry, and narrow-mindedness."

Mark Twain

"Twenty years from now you will be more disappointed by the things you did not do than by the things you did do. So throw off the bowlines. Sail away from the safe harbor. Catch the trade winds in your sails. Explore. Dream. Discover."

Mark Twain

"Perhaps travel cannot in itself prevent bigotry. But, by demonstrating that all peoples cry, laugh, eat, worry, and die, travel can introduce the idea that if we try to understand each other, we may even become friends."

Maya Angelou

"The world is a book, and those who do not
travel read only one page."

Saint Augustine

In the summer of 1972, I began utilizing all I had learned
about flying up to that point to engage in, what to me
was anyway, the motivation behind aviation. I began
preparations for cross-country flying. With each lesson
up until then, whether dual with Mr. Hillman or solo, I
had either practiced countless touch–and–go landings on
Roanoke's two intersecting runways, or I had departed
Woodrum field, flown to a practice area, and then returned
to Woodrum. I developed the skills necessary to safely pilot
the Cessna on cross-country flights, but I was not allowed
to venture beyond the mountains and hills surrounding the
Roanoke area. I was required to stay within twenty-five
miles of Woodrum airport, my safety zone. In doing so, I
learned the names of many of the prominent mountains and
communities encompassing the Roanoke Valley.

Mill Mountain - with its famous centuriate neon star,
Roanoke, Bent, and Cahas Mountains lay to the south and
southwest, as did Twelve O'clock Knob. Poor Mountain,
with its myriad radio towers, and Ft. Lewis Mountain
lay to the west and northwest. Brushy Mountain, Green
Ridge, McAfee Knob, and Tinker Mountain were to the
north and northeast, as was Carvin(s) Cove reservoir. Read
Mountain, Weaver Knob, with its reservoirs atop it, and the
scenographic Peaks of Otter dominated the eastern horizon.
Useful landmarks and checkpoints were located at Montvale
with its many bulky oil and gasoline storage tanks. To the
northeast, up Interstate Highway 81, lay the historic town

of Buchanan – nestled along the James River at the base of Purgatory Mountain. To the west, beyond the city of Salem, were the communities of Elliston and Shawsville; both drew sustenance from Route 11. Southeast of Roanoke beyond Lynville Mountain, Smith Mountain Lake reflected an Old Dominon sky. All of these preadamite Virginian guideposts became salient features in my mind's eye. I grew as comfortable with their friendly and immutable appeal as I was with the scuffed furniture in our den on Brookwood Drive, but I saw them from only one point of view. Like a fledgling sparrow standing on the edge of the nest, I felt the urge to stretch my wings and fly away. As I fluttered around the Roanoke area building solo time, my eyes cast longing glances toward an omni-directional horizon. I yearned for an unfamiliar view of those faithful mountains. I was constantly asking myself, "What's out there over the Blue Ridge?"

In June, my grandparents flew up from Mississippi to visit with us for two weeks. The following Saturday, Dad suggested that we all ride out to the airport to enjoy the afternoon and watch me practice touch-and-go landings and takeoffs. Mr. Hillman had already informed me I was about ready to begin the cross- country portion of my training, but he wanted one more session of traffic pattern practice before I did. The four of them voted to remain in the car up on the road while I walked down the hill to the office. Dad said they would have a good view from there. Shortly thereafter, Mr. Hillman and I taxied out to the runway in 76X to begin the lesson. Along the way, Mr. Hillman leaned close to my ear and warned in a serious tone of voice:

"Now, David, sometime in your flying career you will experience what we call an upset condition while you're on final approach to the runway. Something will happen, such as wind shear, or wake turbulence from other traffic, or a flap may break causing the airplane to skew itself into a dangerous and precarious position. You will need to react quickly to extricate yourself from this condition before the airplane stalls. From that point you'll have about five seconds to continue living. Remember: Power and attitude! Power and attitude! Power and attitude! Also, if you initiate some action and the airplane reacts negatively to it, then quickly undo what you just did. Remember those things!"

He went on to explain just what should and what should not be done, and in what order. I listened attentively to his instruction.

We took off and continued around the traffic pattern as we had done hundreds of times. While on the downwind leg he said,

"I'm going to take the controls when we get close to the runway, and I'll put us into an unusual attitude. I want you to recover quickly – doing just what I have explained. Okay?"

I answered in the affirmative. But, at the same time, I began to wonder about Mom and Dads' reaction to watching my airplane roll itself into such a rakish position at such a vulnerable locale. I briefly toyed with the idea of telling Mr. Hillman that my folks were down there watching us. But, again, I didn't want to upset the timetable of my training curriculum. So, not having any more time to worry about it just then, I quickly put the thought out of my mind.

We turned onto the final approach leg in a stable, trimmed, no flap condition at eighty miles per hour with the throttle closed. Everything looked good from my perspective. As we neared the runway's threshold over Peter's Creek Road, Mr. Hillman suddenly and forcefully hauled the yoke all the way over to the right while simultaneously pulling it as far aft as it would travel. He stomped the right rudder peddle all the way to the floor. The little Cessna heaved a surrendering sigh as if air was rushing from an airtight Tupperware lid. The stall warning horn began its reedy squall unceasingly as the nose went up, up, and up. The world went sideways in a multi-colored blur. Then it became deathly quiet; all sound curiously vanished. We were only seconds from meeting our Maker at that point.

"Recover!" He ordered, breaking the eerie calm.

I reached instinctively for the throttle and yoke, pushing the throttle lever as far forward as it would go into the panel. The engine roared back to life. At the same time, I kicked the left rudder pedal then torqued the yoke back over to the left while pushing it in to lower the nose. With less than perfect coordination, the Cessna responded quickly to counter the threat. I then realigned the airplane with the runway to complete the touch-and-go maneuver. With Mr. Hillman there beside me, I never felt like I was in any real danger – even though we really were. Too much hesitation on my part would have put us in serious jeopardy. We took off again to practice the maneuver five more times - to the left one time, and to the right the next, before we called it a day.

As we taxied in, my mind returned once more to my parents and grandparents sitting patiently in the car awaiting my cheerful arrival. It was not until Mr. Hillman had endorsed my logbook that I informed him we had had an audience the entire time.

"Holy cow!" He said as he pushed his Humphrey Bogart fedora hat to the back of his head.

"You mean to tell me your family was watching all that circus the whole time?"

"Yes, Sir. I believe they were."

"You should have told me that, we'd have done something else today. You'd better go check on them right now."

"Yes, Sir. I will."

I skedaddled up the hill to the car where the four of them were fidgeting with apprehension. Dad lowered his head so he could bore over the top of his glasses.

"Well? How did it go today?" He probed.

"Fine." I said prosaically. "We practiced bad landing recoveries."

Before that moment, I had never witnessed the pathognomy of adults groaning in perfect unison, except at sporting events when the home team has just lost the game, having missed the last chance to pull ahead for the win. It never occurred to me that my mother – bless her heart, had spent the last thirty minutes with her fingernails buried in the headlining of the car crying and wailing odiously. Dad had attracted quite a crowd standing outside the car with his thunderous shouting, "Get down here!" "Come down right now!" – his arms flailing about. My grandmother had quietly bowed her head and prayed for half an hour. Granddad had taken a firm hold of the headrest in front of him and had begun shaking his head continuously back and forth while reciting the twenty-third Psalm.

"The LORD is my Shepherd; I shall not want…."

Chapter Fifteen

Pencils, Plotters, Flight Plans, and Patience

The following Wednesday, Dad allowed me to leave my job in the plant at noon, and I peddled my new ten-speed bike five miles to the airport. Mr. Hillman had requested that I come out during the week so I could sit down with Mr. Brown to begin the flight plan preparations for my first cross-country flight. My destination was to be the Raleigh-Durham Municipal Airport in North Carolina. Over the course of two weeks I would fly three flights with Don Brown to three separate destinations. If all went well, I would repeat the same three flights solo. The spokes on my bike were just a blur all the way up Williamson Road.

Mr. Hillman was coming in from the practice area with a student when I lowered the kickstand, and he greeted me with his characteristic effervescent wave and smile as they walked toward the office.

"Hello, David. How ya doin, buddy?"

"Good, Sir. I'm ready to get with Mr. Brown." I said.

"Okay, mighty fine. I think Don was gonna be 'round back of the office grillin' hot dogs. You might check."

I stepped out the back door and greeted Mr. Brown. He smiled and offered me two grilled dogs. We sat down at the picnic table in the shade of the dogwood tree while we talked about the upcoming flight. I had never gotten to know Mr. Brown that well; I always flew with Mr. Hillman. However, I had heard nothing but complimentary things from everyone about him. My friend Steve said he wouldn't fly with anyone else but Don.

Don Brown was often uncommunicative. He was neither diffident, nor dull. He was simply a quiet man who could be lost in pensiveness – sitting contemplatively in his white shirt and dark tie. When he did speak he floated nothing but kind words for others. Not one time did I ever see him lose his temper. I do remember turning my head to listen to him give his opinion about one thing or another on those rainy weekends when all the old-timers would gather around the stove to swap flying stories. If you arrived after 10:00 a.m. you didn't get a seat. But they always held Mr. Brown's chair open for him while he was with a student. He was a well-respected gentleman.

We finished our lunch, and Mr. Brown said softly,

"Well, let's go in and start that flight log. What do you say?" "Yes, Sir. I'm ready."

As we headed back through the door I asked Mr. Brown about a weathered gray sandbox I spied hiding under a Lilac bush.

"Aw, some of the kids used to play in that thing around here years ago."

I thought the airport was a strange place to have a sandbox….

We pulled our chairs up to the fold down table in the office and spread a new Cincinnati Sectional Aeronautical Chart across it. I had obtained three discarded charts several months previously, and had studied them hour after hour dreaming of cross-country flying when I should have been sleeping. He stabbed his finger at a yellow blob and said,

"Here's Roanoke."

He showed me how the lines on the map accurately reflected the boundaries of the city proper. Referencing the legend on the front of the chart, he began to explain what all the numbers and letters meant. It occurred to me that always before, I was quickly lost in a fog of mental inanition when it came to numbers and letters. However, I listened attentively to every word Mr. Brown said. In about half an hour we had discussed every aspect of the chart that would pertain to our upcoming flight to RDU (Raleigh-Durham).

Next, he produced a tool that resembled a protractor, which I had become familiar with in geometry class. He referred to it as a plotter. He positioned the plotter on the map to facilitate drawing a straight line stretching from Roanoke's Woodrum Field to the Raleigh-Durham airport. I noticed that the RDU airport was actually located on the Charlotte, N.C. sectional chart, and Mr. Brown taught me how to overlay one chart on another. Using the plotter along with the latitude and longitude lines on the chart, I learned how to find the *true course* of the line I had drawn between the two airports. Then by either adding or subtracting the magnetic variation – shown on the chart as either (W)est, or (E)ast - I produced the *magnetic course* of the line. I was beginning to feel pretty savvy about navigation.

Mr. Brown reached into a box on the shelf and retrieved a rectangular metal object with a round dial on it. At first glance, I thought it was a foot calibrator, and I wondered if he was going to measure my feet….

"This is an E6-B computer." He informed me. "We use it to compute all kinds of factors and equations."

It dawned on me that I had indeed seen one before. Mr. Spock used one from time to time to compute trivial factors such as the time and distance remaining to the vertex of a supernova where the Enterprise and its crew would undoubtedly become space roasts. I silently questioned the supposed acumen necessary for such a nugatory trip to North Carolina….

"First, we'll use the wind side." He said. "This time of year the winds aloft at about three thousand feet will typically average close to fifteen knots out of the southeast. So, we'll say the winds for your trip will be from one hundred forty degrees true at fifteen knots."

He had me turn the rotating scale around until '140' was beneath the 'true index' pointer. Then per his instructions, I took my pencil and made a quick dot on the clear plastic faceplate covering the sliding scale indicating fifteen knots above the little hole in the middle of the faceplate. Next, I was to rotate the disc until the true course was under the 'true index.' I asked him what the true course was, and he suggested I already knew the answer. I looked at Mr. Brown with a stupefied expression. He patiently prodded me with a question:

"Now, where have you seen or heard of *true course* before?"

I searched my Lilliputian brain for just a moment before I happened to look at line I had drawn on the chart. After slapping my forehead to give Mr. Brown my best Lieutenant Columbo look, I volunteered,

"Don't I feel like a Meathead?"

I set the course under the index. Then he said we had to slide the pencil mark to the true airspeed line. That one stopped me cold. I had no idea what *true airspeed* was. Mr. Brown quietly explained:

"True airspeed is the calibrated airspeed of the airplane corrected for nonstandard temperature and altitude. Air density decreases with altitude, as does temperature. So, for an airplane to feel the same pressure differential between the pitot impact pressure and the static pressure at three thousand feet as it feels at sea level it will have to fly faster."

He paused to watch my eyes closely to gauge whether or not I had comprehended any shred of what he had just said. I began to slowly drift away into a mental abscission for a few seconds before I recovered with a response.

"Well, I'm in no *real* hurry to get to Raleigh."

"Look here; it sounds more complicated than it really is." He chuckled.

Mr. Brown went on to simplify the concept of true airspeed for me.

"There is less air up high than there is down low – close to the surface."

I nodded. That much I knew.

"The airspeed indicator needs air impacting the inside of the pitot tube out on the wing in order to do its job. Down low, at a given velocity across the ground, there is a set number of air molecules passing the tube over a given period of time – let's say one second. Up higher, there are fewer molecules of air passing the tube for that same given velocity across the ground during that same period of time – one second. So, up high there is less air pressure pushing against the airspeed indicator needle. In addition, the airplane moves through this thinner air faster than it would move through the thicker air down lower, even though the engine and propeller both are less efficient up higher. Think of it like a knife slicing through water versus a knife slicing through molasses."

"Actually, the airspeed indicator is really accurate at sea level only. The higher you go the less accurate it is. It doesn't measure your *true* airspeed anymore because it doesn't receive enough air molecules to do its job efficiently up high. So, we have to compensate. The way we do that is by simply adding two percent for each one thousand feet of altitude you are indicating to the calibrated airspeed."

I nodded again, beginning to understand somewhat.

"But what is calibrated airspeed exactly?" I asked him still mentally wandering a little.

"Calibrated airspeed is simply indicated airspeed corrected for instrument error and possibly installation error. There's always some play in the reading. At cruise speed the difference is negligible, so don't worry about it."

That one was easier to grab hold of.

"So let's say the indicated cruising speed of the one-fifty is one hundred knots. We'll use knots instead of miles–per–hour. If we're cruising at four thousand feet, looking at one hundred knots on the airspeed indicator, what will our true airspeed be? At what airspeed is the airplane *really* moving through the air?" He asked.

I did the math in my head.

"Well, you said two percent per thousand feet. So, two times four equals eight. And, one hundred plus eight equals one hundred eight?"

"That sounds good to me." Mr. Brown smiled. "But that is simply a rule of thumb."

I was genuinely pleased at myself for learning something solid, something tangible I had not known before. We continued the planning session by factoring the estimated groundspeed, wind correction angle, compass heading, estimated time en route, and estimated fuel burn for the flight.

Next, Mr. Brown laid the chart before us again and asked me to mark the checkpoints I would use. I traced the pencil line I had already drawn on the map and marked several features I thought might be noticeable from three thousand, five hundred feet in the air. The first one was easy: Mill Mountain. We would pass just to the east of the mountain with its big metal star. The second point I charted was the sleepy village of Burnt Chimney. I was familiar with the community because I had visited the Booker T. Washington memorial near there. With the groundspeed I factored using the E6-B, we'd reach Burnt Chimney eleven minutes after takeoff. The next was the western edge of Smith Mountain Lake; we would pass along its western boundary edge. Route 40 followed shortly thereafter. Our route would take us over an historic wide spot in the road called Union Hall.

I continued plotting fixes until I had reached the city of Durham, N.C. From its northwestern - most edge, the airport lay hidden in the pine trees fourteen miles further to the southeast and would require eight minutes to reach. In all, we would require one hour and five minutes to complete the one-hundred-four nautical mile trip – with a ninety-four knots per hour groundspeed. We knew the exact time after takeoff we would arrive over each plotted checkpoint. We would burn over seven gallons of gasoline; and with the current oil consumption rate of the airplane, we'd expect to add one half quart of oil to bring the level back to seven quarts after landing at Raleigh.

I had never planned anything in my life in such detail except the pseudo - radio drama, "Shootout At The Not So Okay Corral" my sixth-grade teacher, Mrs. Rouchfort, had us produce as a class project that year in Houston. The thought of venturing beyond my twenty-five mile comfort zone did make me a little nervous. But I was ready to go, to see, and to do. Mr. Brown seemed ready for the trip. He said the airport café in Raleigh had good North Carolina style barbeque sandwiches. We scheduled the flight for the following morning at nine o'clock.

Part Two

The next morning Mom prepared a special breakfast of scrambled eggs with diced sausage and pancakes topped with real Vermont maple syrup. I think she was a little apprehensive about seeing her youngest son fly a little airplane so far away from home. It was her way of giving me my last meal. Dad reassured her that everything would be fine with my instructor with me, but I don't think it soothed her anxious concern.

Dad dropped me off at the airport at eight o'clock. By nine, Mr. Brown and I were ready to go. We started the engine of the newer 1967 model Cessna 150, N6764F, and taxied the little red and white vagabond to runway '23' for takeoff. As soon as we left the ground Mr. Brown told me to note the time. It was 9:20. We would be passing Mill Mountain in three and one half minutes.

It is very difficult to communicate to a non-flyer the thrill and exhilaration a pilot feels when he is heading out across the open countryside to a destination of his own choosing. The aphorism, "Free as a bird" has real meaning and purpose to a pilot flying his own aircraft for pleasure. Piloting airplanes for a living has its own rewards, but that type of aviation isn't really flying at all. Commercial flying is actually air commerce. It's a business. As a commercial pilot, you go where you are told to go, when you are told to go, how fast, how high, and for how much. When you fly large airplanes for a paycheck every month you never hear the words: "Radar service is terminated, have a good flight." You never get to pick your destination – perhaps on a whim. It seems blatantly paradoxical that the very nature of flying, with its three-dimensional freedoms, should be so restricted by statute and decree.

Climbing into the hazy summer morning we slipped by the town of Vinton, cruised over the foothills southeast of Roanoke, and headed out across the verdant Piedmont toward a world I had never seen before. About then the radar controller called us:

"Cessna 6764 Foxtrot, you're leaving my airspace to the southeast. Radar service is terminated. Have a good flight."

With those few words came a new and even more exhilarating rush. From that moment on, I was an explorer charting new lands and experiences. The feeling was similar to the heady thrill I felt when, with my father's help, I rode my bicycle for the first time without training wheels. I had 'it'. Moreover, I would never lose it.

At precisely 9:31, eleven minutes after takeoff, I confirmed the passing of route 122. There was Burnt Chimney. Mr. Brown gave me an affirming nod then returned his gaze to the earth below. Just west of our position was the Booker T. Washington National Monument. I recognized the placement of the restored farm buildings on the scenic grounds. Briefly, I thought about the man:

It was repugnant to me that a youngster could be born into slavery and live such a torturous life simply because his skin was the wrong color. How overwhelming it must have been to this man whose I.Q. was much higher than my own to attempt to overcome such deeply seeded preconceptions as racial bias and bigotry. Could he ever have conceived the idea of viewing his childhood home from the vantage point I now commanded? If he did, could he ever have conceived the idea of being allowed to? It brought to mind a pivotal incident I had witnessed two years before.

My father enrolled my brother in a driver's education class being taught by a private company in Roanoke. Dad wanted to ensure he would pay the lowest insurance premiums possible before Bill got on the road. On the day of the enrollment, I accompanied the two of them to the business office. Dad and Bill were sitting at a desk completing the necessary forms when a well-dressed, very polite black couple entered through the doorway with their son, also needing driving lessons. The owner of the business promptly intercepted them at the doorway and informed them that the remaining classes for the season were already full to capacity. He told them it would be a while before an opening for their son would be available. It was a far different story from the one I had heard only minutes before. The couple lowered their heads in quiet resignation. They understood all too well the injustice that was being forced upon them and their son. They did their best at smiling to thank the owner for his time, and then they turned away to leave. I happened to catch the young man's crestfallen eyes as he looked across an empty room. In them were more than tears. I saw hopelessness. I saw pain as I had never seen before. And I felt disgust for humanity.

Having been born in Mississippi, I grew up seeing and hearing racial bigotry from white people toward black, and from black people toward white, but I was too young to understand the concept. Now that I was older and could be emotionally swayed by viewing it firsthand, I was repulsed by the ugly pestilence. Good people were good people. Bad people were bad people. It was that simple. Color had nothing to do with it. Why couldn't everyone understand that? It was Moses who said, "All who thirst for justice are welcomed in the house of God…."

"Watch your heading there, Dave." Mr. Brown admonished – bringing me out of the mental divarication I had been exploring for a couple of minutes. I had a job to do at the moment, and I needed to pay attention to the business at hand.

Looking ahead, I quickly spotted the next checkpoint – Smith Mountain Lake. We were slightly west of the line we were supposed to be over. I banked gently toward the east to get us back on course. The flowing ripples on the water reflected a shimmering sunlight so that it looked to me like the dancing snow on our television set at home after the station signed off the air late at night.

Smith Mountain Lake, forty miles long with over five hundred miles of shoreline, was created in the early 1960s by the damming of the Roanoke and Blackwater rivers at the Smith Mountain gorge. Gazing downward I could see many boaters and skiers out enjoying the pure waters on the warm summer morning. I knew they were having fun, but I wouldn't have traded places with any of them.

We soon left them behind as our little bird continued on its mission to North Carolina. My watch told me that we should be coming up on the next checkpoint: State Route 40 at Union Hall. I had traveled the highway several times – the last being by chartered bus when my school band entered a state competition in the town of Gretna, about twenty miles east of Union Hall. We placed first in that competition. As the little white country store nestled beside the road at Union Hall slipped by underneath us, I thought about the story of Captain Walter Frederick.

In April of 1865, the boyishly blonde captain from Ohio, along with his company of mounted cavalry, were ordered by Major General George Crook to reconnoiter the countryside southwest of Lynchburg, Virginia after the Union victory at Amelia Springs in order to plot obvious routes of escape by the Confederate Army under General Fitzhugh Lee. The crossroads south of Kaseys, Virginia was their first destination. They were to eventually push westward to the community of Rocky Mount and remain there until relieved. If any Confederate unit was seen marching to the south, Captain Frederick was to send word of it by dispatch rider.

The story has it that Captain Frederick and his men were misdirected, and they ended up spending the remainder of the war bivouacked under the shady poplar trees on top of a hill at a crossroads location between Kaseys and Snydersville. They never did spot the enemy retreating. In fact, it was two weeks after the Confederate surrender at Appomattox Court House before they even received word that the war was over. In the meantime, the Cavalry unit befriended many of the locals, and they all downed much homemade liquor and beer in their tents before they finally constructed a proper saloon for themselves. They named it, appropriately enough, "Union Hall."

It was handed down that other titles for the establishment were suggested by some of the more loyal Southerners, but none of them could be repeated in mixed company. Whether or not this story had any credence, it sounded plausible enough for me to believe.

Seven minutes later we passed route 58 about eight nautical miles west of the town of Chatham, Virginia, where a string of cross-country power lines hung across it. Our route of flight took us just to the east of Brier Mountain. From three thousand feet up it looked like a small hill.

There weren't many distinguishable features in this part of southern Virginia. The terrain held nothing but rolling pastoral hillsides offering a plethora of small farms. At this point it became very important to hold a compass heading accurately and keep a close watch on the passage of time. The visibility had dropped to about seven miles in haze with the glaring sun. About six minutes went by without any identifiable landmarks whatsoever; everything looked the same. I was beginning to squirm a little, and Mr. Brown caught my unease. He'd seen it many times before.

"Just hold your heading. How much time until Danville?" He asked.

"About five minutes." I answered. He seemed satisfied.

I concentrated on holding my heading on 155 degrees while continuing a constant search for other airplanes, but I nervously checked my watch about every fifteen seconds. Even with my sunglasses on it seemed like the visibility continued to worsen. In my mind I could see only about a mile or two. Fortunately, in a short four minutes we began to see signs of urban life ahead. Off to the left, slowly intercepting our route, was the four-lane Highway 29 heading south into Danville. We were on course and on time.

Mr. Brown instructed me to go ahead and call Danville Radio, the FAA Flight Service Station located on the Danville airport, to alert them of our approach from the northwest and passage to the southeast. I snapped on the VHF radio and turned the dial to 123.6 megahertz. Turning in my seat slightly so I could hear my echoed voice off the window next to me, I called,

"Danville radio, this is Cessna, November 6764 Foxtrot, nine miles northwest at three thousand five hundred feet. We'll be passing overhead in six minutes headed southeast to Raleigh, over?"

"Cessna 64 Fox, Danville radio. Roger. No other reported traffic in the area. Altimeter, 30.04. Wind is calm. I'll show your flight plan updated as passing Danville, over?"

"Roger. Thank you. We'll call you at ten southeast of Danville." "Cessna 64 Fox, roger. Is Don with you today?"

At that point Mr. Brown took the microphone and said something to the Flight Service Station employee that I could not hear. There was a genuinely good-natured laugh from the ground and then a polite valedictory.

"Roger, understood. Come see us when you get down this way again, Don. Danville, out."

Mr. Brown smiled as he returned the microphone to its hook. I was going to ask him about the conversation, but I let it pass.

Although uneventful, the remainder of the flight was a bit disturbing for me for two reasons. The first was because the visibility lowered to about five miles with the increasingly dense summer haze. I wasn't used to it at all. The second was because from Danville to Raleigh lay almost nothing but indistinct, monomorphic pastures surrounded by indistinct, monomorphic pine trees. All the checkpoints I had marked from then on seemed indistinguishable and pointless. I determined that if I were going to see anything at all I would have to fly lower. But, I remained at our altitude and held my heading steady on 155 degrees. There was little else to do but wait for the world to pass. I was very grateful that Mr. Brown was with me. We flew on, and in about twenty minutes the city of Durham, N. C. appeared like magic in the windshield. My confidence jumped by leaps and bounds. We had only eight minutes to go.

We landed at the Raleigh-Durham airport at 10:28 in the morning. After parking on the ramp, an affable young lineman helped us tie the airplane down and asked if we needed anything. Mr. Brown requested he top off the tanks so we could check to make sure our estimated fuel burn had been accurate. He returned with the fuel truck and pumped a total of seven whole gallons in the tanks. We walked inside the line office and paid two dollars and sixty cents for the fuel. Then Mr. Brown said it was time for lunch. As we strolled across the terminal apron to enter the building, I stopped to watch a Piedmont Airlines Fairchild turbo-prop airliner land and taxi by – its high-pitched Rolls Royce engines whistling stridently. I wondered how many times I had seen that same airplane in Roanoke.

Our little Cessna was slow compared to many general aviation airplanes. But still, we had arrived at the Raleigh airport only slightly more than one hour after taking off from Roanoke. By car the same trip would have required an exhausting three and one half hours on dangerous two-lane highways. I had enjoyed breakfast at home, and now here I was about to enjoy lunch in Raleigh before noon. There was something to this flying game. I felt special – like I had just discovered a coveted treasure that only a privileged few had ever found. We sat down at the counter and were welcomed by a polite woman about Mr. Brown's age. Her dark hair was tied behind her head in a bun.

"Well, look who's back to Raleigh. Hey, Don; haven't seen you around here for a few weeks. How are things in Roanoke?" She inquired.

"Hey, Peg. This is my first dual back to Raleigh in a while." He said.

Mr. Brown introduced me to the waitress, Peggy Wilkins, and she asked me about flying, my family, and school. She seemed sincere. They proceeded to carry on a cordial conversation – catching up on old news. I was beginning to think Mr. Brown knew everybody east of the Mississippi River. He was genuinely concerned about her mother, and she asked about his. Listening to them talk so easily helped me to relax a bit. I spun around slowly on my stool and drew a deep breath of contentedness. Southern hospitality exudes tranquility. As I used to hear in Mississippi, we enjoyed the backwater shade.

We soon finished lunch and said our goodbyes, and then we climbed the stairs to the weather office to check on the return flight conditions. Next to the landing at the top of the stairs was a large room that had been converted into a museum. It caught my eye, and Mr. Brown told me to have a look around while he continued down the hall in search of a friend of his, a meteorologist.

The walls and partitions of the historical gallery resembled Mr. Hillman's office with its many model planes and photographs on display. There were separate sections for each American war along with one area set aside for civilian aviators of esteem. Of course, Orville and Wilbur Wright were featured prominently. Another section was dedicated to women aviators who had contributed to the birth and viability of aviation in North Carolina. My eyes were drawn almost immediately to a photograph of Louise Thaden standing standing next to another woman I did not recognize, Ruth Nichols. They were posing beside a Beechcraft Staggerwing airplane. The date was 1938. I didn't know any women pilots. I had never heard of any before I started flying lessons except Amelia Earhart. But I was beginning to understand that women had been playing an important role in aviation since many years before I was born. I determined that I would, the very next Saturday, broaden my investigation of the early years of aviation.

We filed our return flight plan and headed back to our Cessna. Mr. Brown said we would use a new tool along with my original flight plan information for our return leg. This was my first introduction to "VOR," Very High Frequency Omni Range navigation.

After takeoff from Raleigh I leveled the Cessna out at four thousand five hundred feet over Durham. Mr. Brown then switched on the navigation radio. I held my altitude and heading rock steady while he dialed in the frequency of the Raleigh range, 117.2 megahertz. He then turned the small knob, rotating the compass card encircling the indicating needle beneath the glass-covered instrument. He stopped with 331 centered under the indice. Mr. Brown brought to my attention the small white needle hanging straight down between a blue inverted arc on the left and a yellow one on the right. The needle cut right through the center of a small white circle between the two colored arcs.

"What this is telling you is we're located on the three hundred thirty-one degree radial of that omni station. The station sends out three hundred sixty separate beams, or radials – one for each degree in a circle." He said.

"With this rotator knob you can tune all of them - one at a time." I nodded vaguely, but I didn't really understand the concept. He continued.

"See this centered needle?" He asked as he pointed. "Yes."

"Watch what happens when I rotate this knob." He turned the little knob slightly counter-clockwise until '300' was centered under the indice.

"See the needle move off to the left?" I nodded again.

"What that is telling you is the 300-degree radial is off to your left." He then returned the rotating card to the 331 position. The needle returned to center.

"See this little flag down here?" He pointed to a small window inside the instrument case. On the tiny flag in the window was printed the word 'FROM.'

"This flag says you are flying away FROM the station, and the centered needle says you are flying on the 331 radial of the station. So, together, needle, flag, and frequency, you need all three, you are flying this airplane 'FROM' the 'Raleigh VOR' station, 'ON' the 331-degree radial. He pointed to each as he spoke.

I was beginning to get the idea.

"How do I change radials? I mean if I wanted to fly on the 300-degree radial to Roanoke how would I do that?"

"You couldn't." He said. "Look at this chart. See the station here at Raleigh? Now look at this blue compass rose around the station. See all the numbers around here? Those numbers are magnetic degrees."

He used the plotter to mark a straight line from the center of the Raleigh VOR compass rose to the Roanoke airport. Then he said,

"Now, look here. We're flying on the, well, let's see. We're drifting east a little. The winds have changed."

Mr. Brown rotated the knob just a bit until the needle centered again.

"Now we're on the 333-degree radial. If you maintain a heading, roughly three hundred twenty-eight degrees or so to allow for wind drift, you would be able to keep this needle centered as long as we were receiving the station. The higher you are the further away you can receive it. Very High Frequency transmissions are what they call 'line of sight' transmissions. He continued.

"Let's assume that we could receive the Raleigh station all the way up to Roanoke at this altitude. If we stayed on the 333-degree radial, where would be after we had flown one hundred four nautical miles?"

I studied the chart and the Raleigh compass rose. The line he had drawn passed through the Raleigh compass rose at about the 328 degrees mark. The 333 degrees mark was five degrees to the right of it. I followed this new imaginary line up to Roanoke.

"Looks like we'd pass somewhere around ten miles east of Roanoke." I answered.

"Yes, about eight to ten miles or so." He confirmed.

"What is the *only* Raleigh VOR radial that passes directly over the Roanoke airport?" He asked.

"That's it, isn't it? I said as I put my finger on the pencil line on the chart while correcting for the one hundred plus feet in altitude we had recently gained. The '328' radial?

You'd be about as right as you could get." He replied. "You could fly on the 300-degree radial if you wanted to, but it wouldn't take you to Roanoke. It looks like it would take you south of Salem at its closest point to Woodrum Field."

For the next half hour Mr. Brown explained the details of VOR navigation. After I got the hang of it, the system seemed much easier to use than attempting to hold a heading while "white eyeing" the second hand of my grandfather's antique stopwatch. About half way between Danville and Union Hall I asked him about locating my position utilizing the VOR radio. The needle told me what line I was on but not the exact position on that line.

"That'd be real easy if we had DME equipment on board. But we don't have it." He pined. "DME stands for Distance Measuring Equipment It measures how far you are away from the station automatically."

"How's your math?" He asked.

"This year we get into advanced addition." I returned ruefully.

"I think you can handle it." He jeered with a smile.

"If we had two of these," He said as he pointed to the navigation radio, "It would be easier to keep tabs on our position. You would simply tune in another VOR station like Lynchburg here, rotate the tuning knob until the needle centers, and then you could see the radial we're on. You use the cross bearings to locate yourself."

Mr. Brown then tuned the radio to the Lynchburg, Virginia VOR frequency, 109.2 megahertz. After he centered the needle with a 'FROM' indication, he said:

"See? We're on the Lynchburg 217-degree radial. If we wanted to fly to the Lynchburg station what magnetic course would we follow, two-seventeen?" He asked cagily with one eyebrow raised. I sensed a trap.

"Well, we wouldn't want to fly a heading of 217 degrees, because that's going to the southwest. And we're already southwest of Lynchburg, right? That would take us away from the station, wouldn't it? I offered.

"That's right. So what approximate heading would you want to fly?"

I had to use the Lynchburg compass rose printed on the chart to help me. I knew we'd need to fly a northeasterly heading. Opposite '217' on the rose was '037'.

"I guess we'd fly a heading of zero three seven?" I cast.

"That's right again. If we wanted to fly to Lynchburg, we'd rotate this knob until the needle centered with a 'TO' indication, which is about 037 degrees. Then we'd turn the airplane to 037 degrees and simply keep the needle centered as we flew along. We'd eventually fly over the station.

Think in broad terms first: North, South, Southwest, and so on."

He continued with some fairly difficult formulas:

"Suppose we didn't have a map. Here we are somewhere between Danville and Roanoke. If the visibility happened to be downright lousy, and you couldn't see more than a mile or two, how could you tell how far away from Lynchburg you were?"

"I have no idea." I said with discomfort as I watched another Cessna pass beneath us headed east.

"Here's how. You just hold your heading for Roanoke while I do this." He instructed.

Mr. Brown centered the needle, and the indice said we were passing through the 225-degree radial of the Lynchburg VOR station. He started his stopwatch. He then rotated the knob until 235 was under the indice. The needle swung way over to the right and stayed there for about two minutes before it gradually centered once more.

"There!" He exclaimed as he clicked the watch again to stop it. "It took us about two and one half minutes to cover ten degrees of change. Now watch." He said.

He took out his pencil and scribbled some figures on his note pad.

"What did we say our true airspeed would be for this leg, one hundred nine knots? And it took us two and a half minutes to cover that ten degrees of change." He said as he pointed rearward. "So, one-oh-nine, times two-point-five, equals what, two-seventy-two- point-five? Two-seventy-two-point-five divided by ten equals twenty-seven-point-two-five, right? So, we're exactly twenty-seven and one quarter nautical miles from the Lynchburg VOR. It's pure magic."

That wasn't all. He had more.

"I plotted the locations on the map where the needle centered both times. The distance we covered in those two and one half minutes was four and one half nautical miles. Remember, keep *nautical* nautical. And keep *statute* statute. The two shall never meet."

He did some more scribbling.

"Distance, four-point-five divided by time, two-point-five equals rate, one-point-eight. So there we have it. We're traveling one-point-eight nautical miles per minute across the ground. One-point-eight nautical miles per minute across the ground times sixty minutes in an hour equals one-hundred-eight nautical miles per hour. So, you can see we're doing one-hundred eight knots across the ground. The winds have changed on us. We don't have our tailwind, but we don't have much of a headwind either. Your magnetic course back to Roanoke from the Danville VOR was what, about 330? You've been holding a heading of about 325 the whole way back, so which way is the wind coming from?"

As a best guess I pointed to the left - westward, but I was beginning to feel very tired. I didn't want to admit it, but I was glad we were nearing a landing at Roanoke. I had almost reached my limit with numbers and letters.

"Yep. We have a left crosswind slowing us down just a little bit." He said, still exhibiting boundless energy.

"Now. What is our groundspeed? What did we say it was a minute ago?" He asked.

I answered. "One-hundred eight knots."

"Okay, again." He continued. "How many miles per minute is that?" He chuckled.

I was beginning to feel somewhat like an over-burdened ox. Even though he had just explained it, I couldn't remember much of anything he had said only a few minutes before. I tried to do the math in my head, but things seemed to be piling up on me. I couldn't concentrate anymore on mental exercises. All I could come up with was a blundering,

"One, uh…."

Mr. Brown sensed my somnolence and calmly scribbled the figures on his note pad once more. Then he went on to generalize the procedure. "Just remember sixty is one mile, one-twenty is two, and one- eighty is three. That's as fast as you'll be going for a while anyway, one-eighty. And it'll be long time before you do one-eighty."

I watched a fleecy white cloud drift slowly by just to the left of us and tried to imagine it passing at 180 knots….

"Another time I'll show you how you can mathematically figure out a three degree descent slope from your cruise altitude as you come in to land at an airport, by multiplying the total altitude you need to lose by three, and then utilizing that miles-per-minute figure. I'll give you some practice math problems you can take home and work on in your spare time. But, I think you've about had enough for one day." He said with a big grin. "Let's just enjoy the scenery on the way in."

I was fascinated by everything he had taught me, but my brain had reached the saturation point, which for me was just above drought level anyway. It was time for recess.

We crossed the sylvan ridgeline south of Vinton and descended into Woodrum field to complete my first cross-country flight. That night I went to bed early – exhausted from a mental overload produced by too much engine noise, Mr. Brown's verbosity, the inability to assimilate information as quickly as it was being delivered, and the release of heretofore-unrecognized tension. As I lay quietly in the dark listening to the crickets outside my window, it suddenly dawned on me why Mr. Brown often seemed so laconic. When he needed to talk in order to teach a student something important, he talked incessantly. By the time he got back to the office his tongue was tired. I smiled a big smile. "Mr. Brown, I know your secret…."

There were many technical factors to resolve about the trip in the days that followed. I had to learn to put into practice all of the procedures and formulas Mr. Brown taught me. However, the most important aspect of the trip for me was the gift of time, if only brief moments, with the people I met. The airplane allowed me to enjoy some free-spirited adventure on my way to creating history with people I had never met before that day. And that was pretty cool.

I never saw the waitress again – Peggy. But I thought about her young son with a weak heart. Her kindness and generosity reflected a gentle soul. She piled that wonderful North Carolina barbeque on our sandwiches higher than anyone else's in the restaurant while we were there; she didn't see that I noticed. The portly silver haired man with the red face and hearty laugh in the weather office at the Raleigh airport was a good storyteller. His name was Givens.

Chapter Sixteen

Now Is Then, Then Is Now

"Strange isn't it? Each man's life touches so
many other lives. When he isn't around he
leaves an awful hole, doesn't he?"

Clarence Oddbody A.S. II

The first drop of salty sweat trickles down to the tip of my nose and hesitates like a reticent child peering into the deep end of a swimming pool for the first time. It then dives to the ground below, whereby it instantly forms a miniscule pool of mud in the powdered soil. The expansive shadow beneath the live oak where I'm sitting, the only shade within a half-mile radius, does little to allay the humid mid-morning heat, which seems to siphon all my energy. The air is still; there is no movement. There is no sound except the incessant buzzing of iridescent flies and the shrill warbling of the katydids in the branches above me. The gravel farm road one mile south of Highway 8 at Dockery, Mississippi is deserted and lonely. Staring across a perpetual emerald sea, I wonder how many well-respected Blues musicians had toiled on this Dockery Plantation cotton field for decades before they were discovered for their musical talents instead of their strong backs. How many had been called on to wage

164

war with primitive tools against such a miniscule and elusive enemy as the boll weevil?

I stepped out of the car and told Granddad I'd be in no hurry to leave. I would sit under the tree and wait for Uncle Bernard to arrive. I didn't want my grandfather to rush, taking unnecessary chances with the car while he ran his errands in Cleveland, ten miles west of Ruleville. His eyesight wasn't what it used to be. I watched him pull away, down the dusty delta back road, and then I found a grassy spot in the shade – my camera ready. My uncle would soon arrive with a new type of tool for killing. This would be a weapon of mass destruction. Minutes after his mission was completed thousands would be dead. And I would witness the carnage.

My eyes searched the distant northwestern horizon for any sign of the big gray and yellow bi-plane. Soon, its familiar silhouette appeared just above the trees about three miles away. In a very few moments I heard the unmistakable throaty rumble of the 450 horsepower Pratt and Whitney radial engine as it pulled the bomber through the air toward its target. The Pegasus approached with swiftness and unwavering purpose. It followed an inalterable path toward the near corner of the field. At the last second it banked hard left to align itself with the first course and dived steeply at the edge. As the snarling nemesis crossed over the power lines at the threshold of the cotton field, a broad sheet of white vapor, wider than the wingspan of the plane, fell airily from behind it and settled uniformly to the ground – only a few feet below.

Rapidly nearing my shaded vantage point, the growling engine, combined with the near supersonic snap of the propeller tips, caused me to cover my ears in an involuntary response. My whole body trembled as the big Grumman Ag Cat roared past, its thick wheels barely skimming the tops of the camouflage that could no longer conceal the enemy. I listened as the translucent blanket of liquid death settled into the field with an ominous eerie hiss. Soon, all insect life before me would be destroyed. The harvest would be saved. Commerce would be defended from nature one more year.

Upon reaching the end of the field he pulled hard left into a graceful climbing turn before banking around to the right in order to realign his airplane for the second pass over the cotton. His skill and perfect coordination had always impressed me, and I wondered at times if I had what it took to be successful at crop dusting, or, as they were beginning to call it, aerial application. It was dangerous work; hundreds of pilots had been killed over the years whether by fate or by a simple moment of inattention. As I watched him line up for his second run over the field I remembered the story Uncle Bernard told me about how he worked his way into agricultural flying. It was an adventure that held me spellbound as a youngster, and I couldn't wait to get flying myself after I heard it for the first time…

Part Two

"In early 1954, at twenty-seven years of age, I was working at Baxter Laboratories in Cleveland, Mississippi mixing and preparing chemical compounds for the injection molding machines they used to manufacture plastic medical products for hospitals and clinics. I had already earned my

Private Pilot's license at the Cleveland airport – a small, dual-runway, grass field in the heart of the Delta region. Mr. Henry Elliot, a soft-spoken gentleman who helped pioneer crop dusting in Mississippi back in the 1920s, taught me how to pilot an airplane just as the Wright brothers had taught him. After receiving my license in 1953, I continued on with my training and earned a commercial license in late 1954.

"I had always been fascinated with airplanes and flying, and having grown up on a farm I knew I wanted to enter professional agricultural flying for a living. So I began working for Johnny Dorr in Merigold, Mississippi during my vacations from Baxter Laboratories – helping out around his 'ag flying' school doing odd jobs in the maintenance shop to pick up some flying time in a Piper Cub. Johnny was an iconic aviation figure both during and after WWII. He founded the first agriculture flying school in Mississippi in the late 1940s. It was from there that I first began spraying crops in the spring of 1955 in a converted J3 Cub. Johnny had removed the front seat and constructed a plywood tank to mount in its place. The pilot flew from the rear seat – just like in most any other tandem seat, tail wheel airplane.

"A few weeks went by and Johnny decided he would let me start spraying poison on some cotton fields between Merigold and Shelby in one of his Stearman Biplanes. These were converted World War II trainers equipped with 225 horsepower Wright Whirlwind engines that he used to teach his Ag students in. They were reliable because they hardly ever broke down, but they were also somewhat under-powered for hauling heavy loads out of short grass strips and maneuvering close to the ground on those steamy Mississippi Delta days. It was while flying Johnny's Stearmans that

I learned the importance of keeping the ball centered in the race while turning; coordination on the controls was imperative. Some of my peers didn't learn that before they augured in.

"Back during that time most agricultural spraying outfits were more akin to gypsy barnstormers than they were fixed-base companies. They'd set up operations and start spraying in the early part of the year way down south in Texas or Florida. Then, after the days became warmer and longer, they'd pack up and work their way north to Louisiana, Mississippi and on up the river valley toward Illinois and Ohio as the planting seasons became optimal for the specific areas. One of these traveling concerns was based in Mercedes, Texas, an agrarian, one-horse town ten miles north of the Mexican border – not too far west of Brownsville. One of the men who owned and operated it, Glen Accord, partnered with a friend of Johnny's from Shelby, John Robert Hollingsworth, in 1955 to buy a spritely, rebuilt Piper Cub sprayer for John to fly up in Mississippi. It was a late model Cub with a larger, more powerful 125 horsepower Lycoming engine installed in place of the original 65 horsepower Continental engine. This arrangement insured the airplane had a lot better performance, but it also made it nose heavy. All-in-all, it was a much better airplane for John Robert to fly doing agricultural work in Mississippi, but it was sitting in a hangar in south Texas. So they had to figure out who was going to fly it up north to Shelby.

"John Robert knew me and my situation – I had just started my vacation from Baxter and would do just about anything to get in the air – so he called me that afternoon at

Johnny Dorr's field and asked if I'd be interested in flying his new J-3 duster back to Mississippi from South Texas. There wasn't any money in it, but he also said he'd let me fly it in spraying operations some if I did. Well, without hesitation I jumped on the offer with a very enthusiastic "yes." He gave me a few details about the flight over the phone, and said Glen would send me an airline ticket to Mercedes as soon as he could. I don't think I slept a wink for the next three days.

"Long about mid-morning on the next Saturday, Daddy and Momma drove me all the way up to Memphis, Tennessee to catch the flight to Houston, Texas, where I was to change planes for the final leg down to Brownsville. From there I'd either hire a taxi or ride the Greyhound the last few miles west to Mercedes. We had thought to give ourselves plenty of time so I wouldn't miss the flight to Houston, but when I checked in at the Trans Texas ticket counter the lady told me that it wouldn't depart until two o'clock in the *morning* and not at two o'clock in the *afternoon*. Turned out that Glen Accord was a very frugal man who wanted to save thirty-five dollars by buying a red-eye ticket – which was fine for him because he wasn't going to be the one boarding the plane. I made my connection in Houston at about twilight on that Sunday morning and arrived in Mercedes before noon on a bright, blue-sky day.

"I didn't spend any time in Mercedes because, when I arrived at the field just south of town I saw some fellows already had the airplane out of the hangar sitting in the grass; it was fueled and ready to go. Glen and another partner of his were there waiting for me, and about the third question Glen asked me was where I intended to land first for fuel. I was familiar with the range of a normal J3, about 160 miles with no wind, and I had thought I'd make the first stop someplace south of Houston. What they told me set me back on my heels. Glen said due to the bigger engine and a smaller fuel tank, this airplane had a range of barely over ninety miles in a calm wind – or just over an hour's worth of flying before I'd have to land for fuel. His partner then spoke up and said not to worry because they had been generous enough to install a reserve gas tank for my benefit – a five-gallon Western Auto jerry can that sat in the empty hopper tank in the front seat. The extra fuel would get me another seventy miles down the road, but I'd have to land somewhere to pour it in the airplane's fuel tank first. Anyway, I had to rethink the entire flight - adding many more fuel stops.

"After squaring things with Glen I loaded my overnight kit in the back and took off from Mercedes headed north for Falfurrias, Texas – what seemed like just a stone's throw up the road. I had drawn a line on my map from Mercedes to Falfurrias and observed there weren't many usable landmarks between the two airports – mostly scrub and bush. VFR charts were notoriously bare of details in the 1950s; however, I saw and circled a couple of grain silos marked on the chart; so I could watch for those in order to check my magnetic course. I was holding a very accurate compass heading for twenty minutes; but even so, the first grain silo never did appear. I climbed higher in an attempt to see further ahead and eventually saw one several miles off to my right – almost ninety degrees. I banked the airplane and headed over that way, but all the while I was wondering how in the world I could have gotten almost eight miles off course after flying only twenty minutes. In due time it dawned on me that the compass was no good at all. It was many degrees off from what it should have been reading. As a result, we [the airplane and me], got back on course about the time I had to land at Falfurrias. I turned around to come in from the east, touched down and taxied to the white-shingled office shack next to the airport rotating beacon tower. Hopping out of the airplane I realized that, this being a quiet Sunday afternoon, there was no one attending the airport to sell me any gas. So I was forced to use the five-gallon can after the first landing.

"The trip continued like that all the way up the Texas coast – watching the section lines, marking off check points, and all-the-while trying to make some sense out of that crazy compass. The only sure way I could identify any particular town was to swoop down and read the name on the water tank. In any event, I made it to Victoria, then to El Campo and Rosenburg, and finally to a small grass field just south of Houston. It was there that I realized I was going need a reliable compass in order to be successful navigating my way across the eastern part of the state with its pine forests stretching for many miles in all directions. The airport manager happened to have one for sale at the counter, so I bought it. He even let me borrow some tools in order to install it myself. After about a half hour I got the thing in okay, but while swinging it to test its accuracy I concluded it wasn't going to work either. There was something in the airplane somewhere causing any magnetic compass to bobble back and forth like a drunken sailor. So, I removed it and took it back to the manager to get a refund, but he said he had just been to the bank deposit box to drop in the take for the day and didn't have any more cash. After a while though, he must have taken pity on me because, between him and the mechanic in the hangar they eventually came up with enough money to give me my refund.

"From South Houston we flew on to Beaumont, Texas where they had a blacktop runway. I refueled the airplane and bought a sandwich and a cup of coffee from the airport café. While there I made careful notations about the course line to my next stop, Jasper. That part of east Texas was flat and featureless; there was nothing but trees for miles and miles. I noticed on my chart that two highways led into Jasper - one from the southwest and one from the southeast. I hoped to arrive over the town right on course, but if I was off, either to the east or west, I'd intercept one of the two highways and follow it to the airport – kind of like a funnel. I took off from Beaumont and circled the field to the southwest. Then I passed over the runway directly on course for Jasper. There would be no more checkpoints until I arrived there.

"The further north and east we flew the hazier it became out ahead of us. The visibility was dropping, and there were several large clouds building off to the northwest through the northeast. I wondered if we would run into rain showers before sunset. I strained my eyes to see ahead, and after a while we came right up on the town of Jasper. I guess fate was with us because we hit the airport on the nose.

"After landing I asked the older fellow who met me to top off the gas. As he did so I reached into the hopper tank, got the five-gallon gas can and set it on the ground to make sure it was full. He saw it and asked what it was for. I told him I needed the five gallons because the airplane's fuel capacity would only allow us to go about ninety miles at a time between fuel stops. He got the same startled look on his face that I must have had on mine when I first heard it, but he didn't say anything. He thought about it for a while though, because while walking back to the office after he was finished he asked me first where I was headed. I told him to Shelby, Mississippi. He then asked me where my next stop for gas would be, and I told him Many, Louisiana and then on to Natchitoches. Those pronunciations were both wrong, and with somewhat of an irritated smirk he promptly corrected me: (Man´-E) and (Nack´-o-dish). He said Many was unattended and didn't have any gas, but that I could land there and pour my five gallons into the airplane tank. He thought that might be barely enough to get me as far as Natchitoches, but he wasn't sure. He seemed very concerned about my future, and he then asked how much total flying time I had. I answered, "Just enough to get a commercial license." Stepping through the office doorway I saw him shaking his head back and forth as if to emphasize what he was probably thinking: "Son, you ain't never gonna make it." At that point I wondered who had more doubt about my success - him, or me.

"I paid him for the gas and headed down the hall to use the men's room. They had a large aeronautical map pasted on the hallway wall, so I stopped and checked my route ahead. There was a pipeline on it running all the way from Jasper to way past Natchitoches that my map didn't have, so I took out my pencil and drew it on my chart. Then I headed back out, took off and got on that pipeline for Many.

"Climbing to about fifteen-hundred feet took a few minutes, and the cooler air was refreshing, but up at that altitude it became evident that the pipeline right-of-way was the only open space in the woods from horizon to horizon. If the engine quit we'd have to land there. The problem with that was it hadn't been cleared; it was logs and gullies from tree line to tree line; no other work had been done. Nevertheless, it was the only way we could go; it was better than flying over solid forest. As we flew on, the haze and cloudiness increased in the late afternoon, and I thought I saw rain up ahead in the murkiness. Sure enough, in just a little bit as we approached the strip at Many, I saw heavy rain coming down in the entire area, and it didn't look like it was in any hurry to move on through. So I turned around and headed back toward Jasper.

"Long about then I started to sweat a little because I didn't have enough fuel left to get there. For just a second or two I thought I was going to be forced to find someplace along that pipeline to set her down and pour in my five gallons, but I suddenly remembered that I had passed over a county highway cut through the trees a ways back. So we continued on southwest until we came up on it after only ten minutes or so.

"From early on in his instruction in flying a student pilot is taught that landing anywhere except an approved airport or landing area is prohibited; the CAA could revoke a pilot's license in a heartbeat for doing so without good reason. All this weighed heavily on my mind as I circled the highway below. The road looked good for a landing; there wasn't much traffic, and it was straight and flat; but I still didn't want to risk a dunking in the hot water I could get into if I got caught landing on it. So even though I was about to have a real emergency I was more scared of landing on the highway. Therefore, maybe against my better judgment,

I continued on towards Jasper until I saw a flat stretch along the pipeline right of way that might give me just enough room to land on and get stopped.

"I didn't have enough time to do a careful survey of the landing area, so I came right around from the west in a steep descent and aimed for the short patch of logging road on the north side of the pipeline that looked clear of debris. There was a temporary power line running across the threshold area, so I had to be fairly aggressive in side slipping it in. I touched down okay, but the red soil was pretty soft. I got on the brakes as much as I could to try to stop her in the short distance available, but with the bigger engine up front I had to be very careful, because the airplane was already nose heavy; I could have flipped her over on her back if had I used too much braking. In the last seconds I saw a gully piled high with logs and cut brush barely a few yards ahead, and I didn't think she was going to get stopped in time before we ran off the edge and plunged down into it. But with just feet to go she hit a softer patch of dirt and came to an abrupt halt. I cut the switch, wiped my forehead and let out a big sigh of relief. I climbed out and checked her over. She didn't seem to have any damage anywhere, so after pouring in the five gallons, I hauled her tail around to the edge of the gully, started her back up and made a short-field takeoff towards the west. We spent that night in Jasper.

"The next day, Monday, was mostly uneventful. We left Jasper in the morning in pretty good visibility and found fuel at almost all the stops we made. I only used the five-gallon can two times before we finally made it back to Shelby. But it was raining pretty hard at the airport there, so I turned around and flew back the few miles to

Merigold and landed at Johnny Dorr's grass field along Highway 61.

"As it turned out, while I was flying back to Mississippi in the new Cub, John Robert broke his hand when the prop on the Cub sprayer kicked back while he was cranking it; he was going to be out of flying for a little while. But that worked out fine for me because my escapade with the big-engine Cub impressed him enough to where he felt encouraged to ask me to fill in for him while he was recuperating. So I had two airplanes to fly during that time I was still on vacation from the job at Baxter. I did okay with all the spraying; the customers seemed satisfied with my work, and that pleased John Robert even more. He soon asked me to continue flying in the evenings after my vacation was over. So I flew all that summer and eventually left Baxter Laboratories to fly agricultural work full-time.

"Every time he'd call from South Texas, Glen Accord would laugh and tease me about my cross-country Cub adventure and if I still had the Western Auto can. Apparently, the whole thing made a good impression on him, too; when the growing season in Mississippi was over that year he called again and asked if I would be interested in flying the airplane back down to Mercedes over Thanksgiving. I told him I thought I might have the time but that I'd have to see about it. I think he could tell I really didn't want to do it, but that didn't stop him from calling me every few days. The thing was, every time he'd call he would change his mind about where he wanted it to go – asking me first to fly it to Mercedes, then to Dallas, then Monroe, then to someplace else I can't remember. I finally told him I didn't want to fly it anymore, and that maybe it was time for someone else to have an adventure of his own."

———————

My uncle had been flying agricultural aircraft for more than fifteen years by the early 70s, and he made a good living doing it. Furthermore, he was good at doing it; he'd yet to have an incident. He never told me himself, but I'd learned some years before that he had won the coveted award of 'Mississippi's Best Aviator of the Year' because of his skill and his sincere consideration for his customers' crops and property. I made it a point to spend some time watching him fly after I had traveled to Mississippi by airline to visit my grandparents during the summer vacations from school. As Uncle Bernard made pass after pass across the cotton that day, my mind drifted back in time. I thought of the genesis of crop spraying. How had history unfolded to bring me to this cotton field on this day, August 17, 1972?

Part Three

In man's quest for technological advantage over his adversaries, it was only a matter of time before the airplane, a neoteric invention in the early 1920s, was staged against the insect, an ageless contemporary. The first such official meeting took place on August 31, 1921 near Dayton, Ohio. Just after dawn, Lt. John A. Macready, an Army Air Corps Officer, took off from an airfield near Dayton in a surplus WWI "Jenny" bi- plane that had been modified to carry a metal hopper tank full of powdered lead arsenate in the front cockpit. Macready's mission was to unload the poison over a grove of Catalpa trees that were being systematically defoliated by an infestation of the dreaded Catalpa Sphinx Moth.

Later the same morning an inspection revealed that all the larvae had been destroyed. Macready, who later went on to test the high altitude superchargers that would power many WWII fighter and bomber aircraft, became an instant hero. Farmers across America took notice; the crop duster was born.

In 1918, an entomologist, Dr. Bert R. Coad, was assigned to research feasible methods to combat the boll weevil. Originally a native of Mexico and Central America, the insect immigrated to the United States in about 1892. It was successful in evading all efforts to halt its march across southern cotton plantations. To expedite his results, Dr. Coad was transferred to the U. S. Department of Agriculture field laboratory in Tallulah, Louisiana. While conducting research there, he met Mr. Collett (C.E.) Woolman, who was a district supervisor for the Louisiana State University's agricultural extension service. Together, the two men experimented with several dry powder insecticides, including lead and calcium arsenate, along with various methods of deploying them. Nothing they tried seemed quite efficient enough at doing the job.

It is interesting to note that both men shared the same passion: flying. C.E. had acquired his enthusiasm for aeroplanes at the first World Aviation Meet in Rheims, France, in 1909. Dr. Coad had developed an interest in flying while in Washington, D.C.

After reading about the successful application of lead arsenate over the Catalpa trees in Ohio, Dr. Coad and Mr. Woolman determined that an aerial application method for their re- engineered calcium arsenate might be the best way to apply the poison to a cotton field. The Department of Agriculture soon dispatched two Army-surplus Jennies to Tallulah, Louisiana - and two Army pilots to fly them. The experiment was an unequivocal success. The boll weevils were dying and the cotton was blooming.

News of the venture spread quickly, and within weeks pilots and farmers from around the south converged on Tallulah – all eager to learn about the new science of crop spraying.

As fate would have it, in 1923, a man by the name of George B. Post, on his way from Texas to Pennsylvania, made an unscheduled stop in Tallulah one day because of mechanical trouble. Mr. Post was a vice president of the Huff-Daland Aero Corp. in Bristol, Pennsylvania, not far from Philadelphia. His company manufactured training airplanes for the U.S. Army. Over the course of two days he became so impressed with the crop spraying operations at Tallulah that upon his return home he persuaded his company to begin producing airplanes specifically designed for the aerial application of chemicals. Huff-Daland set up a subsidiary company in Macon, Georgia the next year - Huff-Daland Dusters. It was the country's first crop-dusting company.

The following year, with C.E.'s encouragement, Huff-Daland Dusters moved their entire operation to Tallulah. This was Mr. Woolman's chance to move into aviation full-time. He resigned from Louisiana State University to accept the position of operations manager and salesman of the new company. Under his guidance Huff-Daland Dusters expanded its operations across the United States in the summer months and into Mexico and South America during the winter. The legend and romance of the daring venture drew scores of free-spirited but hungry barnstorming fliers from across the nation.

In 1928, Huff-Daland Corp. was forced to sell its duster subsidiary due to financial difficulties caused by declining opportunities to operate in South America. C.E. Woolman jumped at the chance to start his own company. With financial help from local investors, Mr. Malcolm S. Biedenharn among them, C.E. set up shop in Monroe, Louisiana. He was at a loss when it came to naming his new venture; however, Catherine Fitzgerald, his young secretary, suggested the name, 'Delta Air Service,' because all of their operations were conducted in the South's delta region. It stuck. Very soon afterwards, Mr. Biedenharn urged C.E. to expand his company into passenger carrying services, which he was eager to do. And within one year the fledgling airline was operating regularly scheduled passenger flights from Dallas, Texas to Jackson, Mississippi with stops in Shreveport and Monroe. Delta Airlines had been born.

The first specifically designed passenger aircraft put into service for Delta in June of 1929 was a Travel-Air Model S-6000-B. The Travel-Air, a five-passenger, 300 horsepower, single-engine high-wing monoplane, cruised at about 130 mph, and had an effective range of around five hundred miles. Prototypes first flew in March, 1925. Delta Air Service purchased three of the craft for its inaugural service. Much of the initial design work on the Travel-Air series was completed by a young engineer by the name of Walter Beech. Before forming the Travel Air Company with Clyde Cessna and Lloyd Stearman, he had been employed by the Wichita Aircraft Company in Kansas. In time, partnered with his wife Ann, Mr. Beech went on to establish the famous Beech Aircraft Company.

Around the same period that the Travel-Air design was entering its initial series of flight tests, Walter Beech befriended a bouncy young tomboy in her second year of college by the name of Louise McPhetridge. Louise was supposedly selling heating oil and building materials for Mr. J. H. Turner during the summer, but she seemed to spend most of her time at the airport making an endearing pest of herself to Mr. Beech. One rainy afternoon, Mr. Turner caught her in an airport hangar with greasy fingernails when she should have been on the road. Instead of firing her outright he took a fatherly interest in her future. He had a lengthy discussion with Walter Beech, and the two men soon made a deal that would allow her to learn to fly and eventually work for a mutual friend, Mr. D.C. Warren, a Travel-Air Dealer in the Oakland – San Francisco area. Her dream had come true; Louise would become a pilot – quite an obstacle for a woman to overcome in 1927.

Over the course of the next few years, Louise not only learned to fly, but she also became a licensed Transport Pilot, set many new speed, altitude, and endurance records, and won two cross country air derbies - including the 1936 Bendix Cup Race - for which she received the coveted Harmon Trophy. On July 21, 1928, she married her sweetheart, Herbert von Thaden, an engineer and Army pilot who, like Mr. Beech, believed the future of aircraft design lay in metal work, not fabric.

Throughout 1929, Louise was employed as a factory representative for the Travel-Air Company. She served in the same capacity for the Beech Aircraft Company from 1937 through 1940. She demonstrated and delivered the Travel-Air S-6000 B, as well as other types, to pilots and managers of many different companies around the country, including those of Delta Air Service in Monroe, Louisiana.

Early during World War II, the Thadens settled in Roanoke to begin a business of their own: Thaden Engineering Company - researchers and designers of various plastic products for military application. While in Roanoke during the war, Herb and Louise Thaden became good friends with Mr. Wesley Hillman and Mr. Boots Frantz. Later they were introduced to Edith after she and Wes were married. They interacted socially as well as professionally.

After the war, Mr. Hillman assumed command of the Southwest Virginia Squadron of the Civil Air Patrol. He was successful in inducting Louise into the squadron shortly thereafter. They flew a number of search-and-rescue missions together before Louise was invited to assist in commanding the National CAP wing in Washington, D.C.

Part Four

Near the turn of the century, about the same time my grandfather was born barely one hundred miles north in Tennessee, a young boy stood staring out across another cotton field near Corinth, Mississippi, and made up his mind that he would follow his passion for fast automobiles and motorcycles instead of his father's footsteps into farming. His name was Roscoe Turner, and he grew up to be an eloquent speaker as well as a compelling persona of aviation in the 1930s. He was a restless young man eager to get out in the world and make a name for himself. He was full of ambition. If Roscoe Turner had had any motto at all it would have been: "Look the part. Dress for success. Be good at what you do, and act confidently."

Turner left home in 1914 to pursue his dream of working on automobiles. He took an ignominious but honest position in Memphis, Tennessee as a mechanic's assistant and truck driver. Believing he should look appropriate for his career, he spent his last few dollars on a suitable uniform so he could impress his customers and his employer. This philosophy served him well all through his life. Roscoe held several jobs while he lived in Memphis until war broke out for the United States in 1917. He had seen his first airplane a year earlier, and he decided he would turn his interest toward aviation.

Not having the education needed to qualify as a pilot for the army, Turner enlisted as an ambulance driver and was subsequently sent to France as a Sergeant. His passion for flying grew, and he eventually received a transfer to the Army Signal Corps where he trained to become a balloon observer; soon after, he was promoted to the rank of second Lieutenant. While serving in that capacity he learned to fly airplanes by taking clandestine lessons from several of his fellow officers in exchange for unauthorized gifts. In his always-immaculate uniform, Roscoe Turner became legendary for wheeling-and-dealing with the local populace for the benefit of his comrades in uniform. If his friends wanted chicken for the evening's meal, Roscoe asked, "Fried or broiled?"

After leaving France in 1919 as a first Lieutenant, Roscoe followed his newly-found passion for flying by teaming up with Harry J. Runser to form a flying circus. Turner did most of the wing walking and parachute jumping for the act across the south and eastern portions of the United States. He also sold rides in their Jenny bi–plane for one dollar per minute. Still a believer in dressing for success, Turner and Runser discarded their army uniforms when they wore out and began wearing their own uniquely designed and very colorful uniforms – complete with insignia badges, Sam Browne belts, polished black boots, and officer-style caps. The uniform became Roscoe's signature trademark for the rest of his career in aviation. To complete the look of the dashing aviator, he grew a mustache waxed into needle points, further enhancing what he called, "my stage smile."

In 1927, in the midst of the Charles Lindbergh frenzy, the flamboyant Turner received his golden opportunity at fame and fortune when he was contacted by an equally sensational young aviator and movie producer, the enigmatic Howard Hughes. Turner had purchased Igor Sikorsky's gigantic S-29A for ten thousand dollars with the help of several east coast financial backers in order to start an airline. Flying between New York and Atlanta, the immigrant Russian designer's Herculean bi- plane could carry fourteen passengers in a comfortably-heated cabin. The airline deal fell through, but Hughes needed an airplane that could pass for a WWI German "Gotha" bomber for his burgeoning motion picture epic, *Hell's Angels.*

....The colorful Turner, decked out in his ostentatious uniform, was greeted with much pomp and circumstance upon arriving in Los Angeles aboard his mammoth airplane. Bound for stardom in Hollywood, Roscoe Turner reveled in the spotlight with many film stars of the day – Jean Harlow, Ben Lyon, and James Hall, to name a few. He instructed several of them in the art of flying. The Hollywood elite seemed to rush to have their pictures made with the dashing aviator. Turner took it all in as "good for business." He was never a fan of the supposed Hollywood lifestyle. In fact, according to those who knew him on a more personal level, Roscoe Turner was a very spiritual man. Not one for regular attendance inside a church, he faithfully read his Bible every night before retiring. A friend quoted him one day to the press: "In His infinite wisdom and goodness, God constantly has an angel by my side watching over me."

Turner's popularity increased again after the MacRobertson Air Race in 1934. Flying a sleek new twin-engine Boeing 247 passenger airliner fitted with extra fuel tanks, Roscoe Turner and his two crewmen – Clyde Pangborn and William Lear, (who also invented the first usable radio direction finder), placed third in the grueling London, England to Melbourne, Australia four-day event. They were the only American flight crew to complete the race. Herb and Louise Thaden had planned to enter the competition flying a specially designed Beech aircraft. Unfortunately, it was not completed in time for them to qualify for the race. It is interesting to note that this same Boeing 247D that Roscoe Turner and his crew flew into the history books in 1934 now resides prominently in Washington D.C.s' National Air and Space Museum.

Roscoe Turner did more than win air races. He charmed the nation when he cleverly adopted Gilmore the lion cub as his traveling companion. Turner had signed a marketing agreement with Mr. Earl Gilmore, president of Gilmore Oil Company, to serve as their official advertising agent. With the lovable cub by his side, Turner crisscrossed the country and made Gilmore's 'Red Lion' oil products a household name. Roscoe and Gilmore, now an internationally recognized duo pictured on the cover of every magazine in the nation, were soon hired by the Heinz 57 Company to give notoriety to their numerous products. As a result, The Roscoe Turner Famous Flying Corps, a promotional gimmick devised to encourage youngsters into aviation as well as move large quantities of Heinz products, was launched in 1935.

In a co-marketing agreement, starry-eyed dreamers all over the country were enticed into clipping and mailing box tops and seals to the company's headquarters in return for badges, golden lapel wing pins, and rank insignias. The more proof-of-purchase seals a Corps member returned to the company, the higher in rank he climbed. Not surprisingly, the sale of Heinz 57 products skyrocketed for several years in a row because of the energized enthusiasm of tenderfooted adventurers. Turner developed a special secret code so each corps member could identify himself as an officiary of the exclusive club. When meeting a higher ranking officer in public, identifiable by his corps wings and insignia badge, a compatriot would snap to attention, cross a two-fingered salute over his heart and announce, "Eleven thirty." The phrase represented Turner's race-winning, east-to-west cross-country flight time: eleven hours, thirty minutes from

New York's Floyd Bennett Field to Los Angeles in 1933. In response, the greeted young airman was to return the salute and reply: "Ten four," Roscoe's mind- boggling record time from west to east across the country, ten hours, four minutes. The fad exploded with such monumental enthusiasm that police departments and law enforcement agencies across the nation eventually adopted the code. "Ten four" became their official acknowledgement code of a message received and understood. The entire nation was mesmerized by the charismatic charm of Roscoe Turner.

. The indelible Mr. Turner continued to transfix impressionable young minds until the beginning of World War II. With its arrival the end of the innocence was near. Nevertheless, he forged ahead and did his part for the war effort by opening a government-contracted civilian flying school in Indianapolis, Indiana. Turner and his staff trained hundreds of young combat fliers; many of the young men had previously been members of his popular pre- war flying corps. He also established a Civil Air Patrol wing in Indiana. After the war, Roscoe Turner served on the House of Representatives Science and Aeronautics committee for more than eight full years.

My uncle made three round trips to the plantation that morning as I watched from under the oak. He had passed over the field more than thirty times dispensing poison to control the boll weevil population. As he disappeared for the last time over the tree line to the northwest, I thought to myself,

"How sad it is to know that Roscoe Turner has passed on a mere two years before; he was such a colorful figure in aviation's past. The old-timers spoke of him often, the ones who were still around…."

Many of the pioneers had gone on: Walter Beech, Clyde Cessna…. I wondered, too, how much longer the gentle and graceful Louise Thaden would be with us. Her husband, Herb, had already left to be with the Lord he loved. He was a good man, a Christian man. So many people in history, so many lives before…. Each had helped shape aviation into what it had become. I realized then that my start into an aviation career would not really be a beginning at all. Like my Uncle Bernard, I would pick up my tools and quietly mold myself into a small link to join an ever-lengthening and indomitable chain.

Looking out across the cotton field, I wondered, too, about the cycle of life. All those insects had been alive just moments ago. Now they were dead. What did their lives amount to? Why did they ever exist in the first place? Were our lives that simple? Were we nothing but soulless insects, alive one day, exterminated the next? Did *we* exist simply to live for the next moment in time? We *had* to be here for some reason. There was an *order* to life – a biosystematic dictum *for all to see*. Order did not simply arise from nothing. Something, or some-*one* must have *created* the order. In the stillness of the sun-baked Delta cotton field, beside that lonely gravel road, I bowed my head and said these very few words:

"Lord, I know you are here, somewhere. In my heart I feel your presence around me. I have no idea what I am to do, but if you'll guide me I'll try to follow your will and not my own for the rest of my life."

It was that simple, but I was changed forever, and I knew it. There could be no going back. I'd fall far from time to time; the enemy within my flesh would make sure of it. It wouldn't matter though. The one who said he would pick me up and dust me off each time I would fall would never leave me.

I spotted the bone-dry dust being stirred by Granddad's white Plymouth Fury as he approached from the west. It was near to dinnertime, and he would be eager to return to Ruleville. I had enjoyed all of the humid Mississippi heat I cared to absorb for one day. He slowed to a stop under the tree, rolled down his window, smiled and said,

"Well, it's almost dinnertime. You think Gramma will have those good ol' homemade chicken and dumplings ready by the time we get back?"

I grinned in return and said, "I'll betcha she will, Granddad."

He looked at his watch and speculated, "It's about eleven thirty. I expect you'd win. Let's get on back to Ruleville."

Closing the door behind me, I looked out across the cotton fields one last time and replied,

"Ten-four, Granddad. Ten-four."

Chapter Seventeen

Over the Blue Ridge Part One

"…Do you think I have come to bring peace to the earth? No! I have come to bring strife and division. From now on families will be split apart - three in favor of me, and two against — or the other way around. There will be division between father and son, mother and daughter, mother-in-law, and daughter-in-law."

Jesus, Son of Man

There had been many changes around our modest home on Brookwood Drive by the autumn of 1973. My sister began her second year of college at East Tennessee State University in Johnson City that September. She was studying to be a schoolteacher. Bill had been drafted into the Army, and he barely missed being sent to Vietnam. President Nixon had already started winding down U.S. involvement by the time Bill was ready to be deployed anywhere. So he spent his enlistment on the bonny beaches of Hawaii as the assistant editor of the post newspaper. Dad finally purchased the type of car he wanted, not the type the family needed, a brand new Oldsmobile 88, metallic lime green. It was the biggest, most luxurious automobile I had ever ridden in. Mom, at the tender age of fifty years, decided to return to school to become a registered nurse. It would take three years of hard work to earn her degree in nursing, but it was something she had always wanted to accomplish.

In August, I passed the Private Pilot flight test with Mr. Hillman. And with my new pilot's license, I began to explore distant horizons. The money I earned at Blue Ridge Steel during the summer and Christmas vacations afforded me the opportunity to unlock the mysteries of the eastern U.S. while having a ball doing it. Because I was a senior that year, and, whether a nerd or not, could legitimately ride in the very back of the school bus, I decided to take 'cool' one step further and use the airplane to help foster my educational objectives.

Coach Hammas, my history teacher at Cave Spring, issued an assignment on a Monday afternoon in middle October with implicit instructions on its completion by the end of the semester, before the Christmas break. We each had to research an event, a person, or a particular place in Virginia's history of our choosing and write a thoroughly exhaustive essay on the subject. Gazing around the room at all of the aggrieved countenances, I contemplated who would be the most exhausted – the writers, or the readers.... The paper would amount to a whopping sixty percent of our final grade of the semester. With so many percentage points riding on this one essay, I figured I could flunk two tests, pass the rest with high 'Cs', and still earn a 'B' in the class if I turned in a classy essay.

History had always been among my favorite subjects, but I believed the manner in which it was dump-trucked onto stuporus high-schoolers was abhorrent. After all, who could possibly get excited about memorizing a list of names and dates, or learning about one worthless treaty after another? History was all about passionate extremes – loss and gain, love and hate, jubilation and despair, conflict and coherence. History was about humans and humanity. History was the very heart of mankind – God's grace and judgment. I determined I would discover something worthwhile to write about – something emotional to many – controversial to all.

That night at the dinner table I asked Mom and Dad what they thought would be a suitable subject about which to write an award-winning essay. After some in-depth discussion, we all agreed I would do well to spotlight an unusual character – a very colorful person who had had a profound effect on American society as well as the course of history in Virginia during a particularly difficult period, such as the War Between the States. Of course, there had been many colorful and acclaimed figures in Virginia's reverential past: George Washington, James Madison, James Monroe, Thomas Jefferson, and Robert E. Lee being the five most recognized luminaries. But I felt that each of them would be well represented by my classmates. I wanted someone who was not so well recognized and respected by high-schoolers from such a bulwark confederate state.

Dad turned the television on while we ate, and the evening news was broadcasting the latest coverage of the war in the Middle East. Israel had been recently attacked by Egypt and Syria during Yom Kippur ceremonies on October

6th. The defiant little bastion nation was fighting for its very survival. Yom Kippur was the Day of Atonement for the Jews. A strike against them at that time touched the hearts of most Americans in the same respect that our own Pearl Harbor was sneak-attacked by the Japanese on a Sunday morning. It was dirty deed by the Muslims; however, I felt that no Islamic country could ever hope to beat the Israelis militarily. Israel possessed dozens and dozens of Fortune Five Hundred companies with the technology and knowhow to build a massive Army and Air Force. The Arabs were at a loss to produce an outhouse with electric power.

Dad observed the progress of the war with an anxious concern, and then he opined that most wars have been fought in the name of God.

"Dave, throughout history, people have been killing and destroying each other – all of it in the name of religion. You can do ANYTHING you feel like want to do and claim it in the name of God, or some god. Even the Muslims with their Satanic god, allah, claim to be doing God's work here on Earth. Most Arabs are cowards anyway. They'll stab you in the back, but they won't stand up against you and fight."

After the segment about the war was finished, Dad slammed his fork down on his plate and exclaimed with much zealousness.

"The Jews are going to kick those Islamic step children back to the stone-ages one of these days. And that won't be too hard because they're only half way out of it as it is!"

Mom flushed at Dad's ungodly fulmination. He was quite emotional when the subject turned to matters of Biblical prophecy and war. Anyway, his disquisition gave me the idea of using religion as the axis of my essay. It all fell together in sequential logic: Biblical prophecy, fanatical and false religiosity, surprise attack, unrestrained battle, profound change, and Virginia history. There was only one man, epicentered in one event, during one particular period in U.S. history who could personify that exact description: John Brown.

Part Two

The clear night was just beginning its retreat as I stood at the apex of our driveway looking east toward a deep purple dawn over the Roanoke Valley. On a good day you could stand so and see the majestic Peaks of Otter, Sharp Top and Round Top. But at this fetal hour they were still cloaked in darkness. George and Jim, my two dogs, sat near me — sleep still heavy in their eyes as they yawned continuously. They were loyal pets, neither of which would ever question my sanity about being up so early on a Saturday. Jim was an intelligent dog who yawned sympathetically if I enticed him so. I never could get George to do it, though; he never caught on. Jim would finally wise up to my antics and look away, but he wouldn't leave my side.

I had everything I would need for the day in my knapsack: ham sandwiches, thermos filled with cold milk, maps, computer, plotter, Boy Scout knife, camera, tape recorder, and notebook. I was reviewing the contents mentally when Steve and Larry came rumbling up the street in Steve's new silver Chevy Camero. Steve had followed his father's footsteps onto the rails of the Norfolk and Western Railroad after high school. It was sound, honest work, soon affording him the opportunity to purchase his dream car. With an affectionate pat for each, I said goodbye to my sad-eyed companions, jumped into the back seat of the car and held on as Steve sped around the curve that crested the hill on Brookwood Drive.

"Hope you've got everything you need 'cause we ain't goin' back. We're a little behind as it is. Jim and Debbie will probably be waiting on us when we get there." Steve announced.

"Nope, I'm all set. Good mornin', Larry. You ready for this?" I asked Too Tall concerning the adventure ahead of us.

"Yeah. Ready to go. You feel well enough to fly today?"

"Oh yeah. It's going to be a day to remember all right." I replied with a big smile.

The three of us had been planning the trip for over a week. We would take two airplanes - one of Mr. Hillman's Cessna 172s, and Bill Saker's shiny new Skyhawk. Steve had checked out on it the month prior. Our destination for that Saturday was Harpers Ferry, West Virginia. The trip was originally my idea. I was going up to do research for my essay on John Brown's raid at the U.S. Armory there in October of 1859. Steve suggested that we take a formation flight up the Shenandoah Valley. He said one of his peers at work, Jim Ewing, told him that he had an uncle who owned a large corn farm near there that had a three-thousand foot grass airstrip on it. As long as he could go along, Jim would see to it that we'd be able to land on the farm - only four miles from Harpers Ferry - instead of the twenty miles to the Martinsburg, W.V. airport, the closest public airport to Harpers Ferry. We all agreed it would be much more exciting to have two airplanes flying together rather than just the one flying alone. Steve would take his friends, Jim and his wife, in Bill's Skyhawk, and I would take Larry with me in the Hillmans' gleaming 172. When we arrived at the airport Jim and Debbie were indeed waiting for us – parked along the road near Bill's hangar.

"Hope we didn't keep you waitin' long." Steve apologized.

"Naw, we've been here since a little before five-thirty, but we couldn't sleep anyway," replied a muscular young man of about twenty-five years. He gave me a firm handshake as he introduced himself and his wife, Debbie.

We made a little small talk, and then Larry and I walked down the taxiway to our airplane waiting for us outside Mr. Hillman's hangar. Jim had been a conductor for the railroad for four years. He and Steve worked together occasionally on local 'way freight' runs up the Shenandoah division line. Debbie was a farm girl from Winchester, Virginia. She and Jim had been married for only a year, but they both said they wanted children soon. Judging from their open honesty and sincere amicableness, I liked them immediately. And I knew that someday they would have a wonderful family. They seemed genuinely friendly and accepting of others.

"Larry, I hope I can find a wife like that one of these days. She seems sure of herself enough that she doesn't need to try to wear the pants in the family, you know?" I said to Larry as we walked.

"Yeah. She seems nice and friendly. They sure look like they're in love, don't they?"

"Yep."

We untied and preflighted the airplane, started her up, and then joined Steve out on the ramp in his Cessna. After doing some coordinating on the radio with the ground controller we taxied together to runway "33," where we each completed our cockpit checks. Steve was the flight leader for the day. Larry and I would follow about three seconds behind. Because we each had two radios, one for ATC and one for plane-to-plane communications, we were able to talk to each other while simultaneously communicating with the tower. Although, as it is normally done in a two-ship formation, I, the wingman, would not be talking to Air Traffic Control. Steve would handle all ATC responsibilities. All I had to do was listen to them communicate with each other and stay in formation with Steve's airplane.

"Y'all ready?" Steve called.

"Affirmative." I said, trying to be professional.

Steve then called the tower for a formation take off clearance.

"Roanoke Tower, Cessna 84352, flight of two, ready for takeoff, departing to the northeast."

"Cessna 84352, flight of two, Roanoke Tower. Cleared for takeoff, wind is calm. Departure to the northeast is approved. Traffic for you is a Piedmont Airlines YS-11 approaching the airport from the northeast, twenty miles out, descending now below six thousand. I'll keep you advised. Over?"

Steve acknowledged the clearance and taxied out into takeoff position on the left side of the runway. I moved into his four o'clock position on the right side of the runway. Looking down the field, I noticed the green and white rotating beacon on top of the tower cab above the terminal was still on; we would be airborne before official sunrise.

Steve went to full throttle and started his takeoff roll. After waiting about five seconds, I completed one final check of the flight controls and did the same. Larry was bug-eyed the whole time.

We had agreed earlier that Steve would lift off and hold his airplane down low to the pavement. My airplane was a little lighter, so I lifted off a little sooner and I climbed slightly higher to avoid the turbulence being created by the Cessna in front of us. Thus set, we climbed in formation into the cool morning air. The sky to the east was quite bright – a promise for a new day. I kept a comfortable distance from Steve, behind and to his right, not wanting to risk a collision.

"I didn't know Piedmont had any arrivals this early." Steve called on the radio.

"Maybe it's a charter, or a maintenance flight." I replied. "Could be."

Far below, the streetlights were beginning to die as we passed south of rugged Tinker Mountain and headed across Botetourt (Bod – uh – tot) County. Without warning, the blinding brightness of the sun's corona broke over the Blue Ridge, filling the cabin with warm light as we crossed over Troutville. The blue sky was streaked with lavish brush strokes of pink, orange, and yellow.

Up to the north, nestled beside U.S. Route 220, lay the small town of Fincastle. It was the seat for Botetourt County. At one time, Botetourt County encompassed the entire area from its present boundaries, south to the North Carolina border, west to the Mississippi River, north to Wisconsin, and back southeast to Fincastle. I expressed this fact to Larry.

"I guess the folks who lived in Illinois had trouble paying their property taxes on time back then, huh?" Larry contemplated.

"Hey." I called on the radio to Steve. "Yo." He answered. "You ever see that YS-11?"

"Naw, I think he passed to the south of us to enter a right base for "33."

"Roger that. Larry says it sure is pretty isn't it?" "Rraahger. I've got a lot of ooooohs and ahhs in here." "I understand. It's a good day for them."

About that time the tower called Steve.

"Cessna 84352, flight of two, Roanoke Tower. You're leaving the airport traffic area to the northeast. YS-11 traffic is no factor. Squawk one, two, zero, zero. Have a nice flight, gentlemen."

Steve replied, "Roger, 84352, we'll see you this evening. Have a good day."

We climbed to three thousand five hundred feet and leveled off, where we each throttled back so we could cruise at a leisurely pace up the valley; we were in no hurry to reach the farm outside Harpers Ferry. The air was perfectly smooth, and the Cessna showed no predilection to wonder off the trimmed heading and altitude. So, I was able to relax and enjoy the view along the way. And what a view it was.

Virginia's mountains in mid-October create a nature lover's paradise. The fall colors are usually peaked at that time. Stretching for miles in all directions, covering the flanks of the immutable mountainsides, are poplars, hickories, birches, striped maples. In fact, there are over one hundred species of trees and shrubs inhabiting the Shenandoah National Park alone. As we winged our way closer to Natural Bridge, the rising sun seemed to set fire to the rolling farmland and hillsides below. Blazing reds, vibrant yellows and oranges, cool greens, and deep purples filled our eyes and minds with reverential awe for such a created beauty which effortlessly surpassed our childlike comprehension. I was humbled simply by the privilege of witnessing such magnificence. Larry and I looked at each other and smiled. Without words we communicated a clear understanding that, together, we were being offered a wonderful but inexplicable gift. We were elated.

"Hey, Dayeve." Steve radioed in his mountain drawl. "Go."

"I'm gonna angle off to the east a little bit and follow the James River up to Glasgow. Jim and I work out of there a lot, and I want him to see the rail yard from the air."

"Okay. We're about a hundred yards behind you, slightly to your right. We'll stay in this relative position. Let me know if you're going to do anything but gentle turns."

"Hey. There's Natural Bridge up ahead to the left. See it?" I called to Steve.

"Yeah, I see the hotel." He said.

Natural Bridge, Virginia – one of the seven natural wonders of the entire world, was once owned by Thomas Jefferson when he purchased 157 acres of land, including the bridge, from King George III of England, in 1774 for a mere twenty shillings, (One pound, or slightly less than two U.S. Dollars). Wealthy Europeans of the 18th and 19th centuries established riding parties and hunt clubs on the grounds surrounding the area as a means to disassociate themselves from the lower classed immigrants of the day as they traveled about the new world. It is said that George

Washington carved his initials, G.W., into the limestone rock at the base of the bridge when he was surveying the area on behalf of Lord Fairfax the 6th in 1750. The bridge, which carries U.S. Route 11 across its ninety-foot span, stands 215 feet high, and was created centuries ago when Cedar Creek, a tributary of the James River, collapsed the cave from which it emerged.

A legend among Monacan Indian descendants tells of a miraculous escape from pursuing Algonquin warriors when the collapse of an impregnable wall occurred suddenly as they knelt and prayed to the "Great God." This timely implosion allowed them to cross the barrier before a chasm was created behind them, blocking the enemy from further pursuit. Clearly, the Hebrews weren't the only recipients of miraculous grace….

"Have you ever been to the Sunday brunch at the hotel in Natural Bridge?" Larry asked me as he watched the bridge slide by on our left.

"Once." I replied. "My Dad took us up there last year. They had good chicken."

"Dave. I'm gonna descend to two thousand feet so we can get a better look at the switching yard." Steve radioed.

"Alright. Go ahead."

I throttled back a little in order to hold a steady position behind the airplane ahead as Steve began a slow descent to two thousand feet. At that altitude we'd be well below the crest level of the Blue Ridge, paralleling our course on the right. The sun glinted off his polished wings on the new heading, so I repositioned our Cessna further to the right, but still well behind. Larry and I both kept a sharp eye out for other traffic.

We intercepted the swift James River where it straightened out south of Salling's Mountain before it turned south to cut through the Blue Ridge at Balcony Falls Gap on its way to Lynchburg. From there we had a clear view of the town of Glasgow and the rail-switching yard.

"Dave, did you know that Glasgow was supposed to be the biggest city in Virginia at one time?" Larry asked me.

"No, I never heard that before." I said.

"Yeah, my Dad told me that years ago. Because of these two rivers, the James and the Maury coming together, and the two railroads that merge here, what now are the Norfolk and Western, and the C & O, several big manufacturing companies relocated to Glasgow in the late 1800s and began selling land and developing property in order to lay out a huge city that was supposed to be bigger than Richmond. He said money rolled in from all over the world – mostly from England. See how the streets are laid out in wide blocks like that?"

I banked the airplane to the left to get a better view of the town.

"Architectural and city engineers planned them that way – just like a big town. But when the economic collapse hit the entire country in 1893 everything went bust, and nothing ever came of it." Larry continued: "He also said that dam down here on the right might be torn down, because everybody claims it causes most of the flooding in this basin area here. The last big flood was just a few years ago in 1969."

We turned to the right so I could see the dam.

"Looks like they're working on it now, doesn't it?" Larry commented as he pointed at the dam.

"It sure does. They're doing something to it. Look at all that heavy equipment down there."

"Yeah. I remember the flood of '69. We moved to Roanoke just a few months before it hit. That all came about because of hurricane Camille wasn't it?"

"Yeah. That was a bad one. It went all the way up into Ohio and Pennsylvania causing all kinds of destruction."

About then Steve called again.

"Hey, we see the office shack where we sometimes eat lunch. It's that blue brick building down there next to the parking lot with all the truck trailers in it. See it?"

"Yeah, we see it. Is that your mess back there behind it? Looks like a trash dump. Don't you guys ever pick up after yourselves?"

"Ah, they throw all the cardboard and wooden crates back there during the week, and then some guys from the paper company come around on Wednesday to pick it up." Steve explained.

Our pair of Cessnas climbed away from the sleepy town of Glasgow and headed northeast toward our next checkpoint – the Highway 60 overpass at Lexington and Buena Vista. The air was still very smooth, and 23Quebec handled like a charming lady on my arm. I could delicately pressure her in the small of her lovely back toward the desired direction, and she responded with an aristocratic composure – her pretty head held high. Gazing down upon the cars on Interstate Highway 81, I momentarily felt a smug vaingloriousness at my ability to sail swiftly over the earth-bound urchins crawling along behind the soot-stained eighteen-wheelers in front of them. However, just as suddenly, my self-derived augustness was notched back to reality.

"Well, Dave, at least those people down there can afford to buy their own cars – which is more than you can do." I said to myself. Sometimes your conscience has a clever way of keeping you in your place.

As we cruised through the waxing October morning, five explorers seeking new adventure, we passed the historic town of Lexington, Virginia, the home and final resting place of General Thomas "Stonewall" Jackson. He was immortalized at the first Battle of Manassas, in July 1861. It is also the home of his beloved Virginia Military Institute, upon which he left an indelible impression.

From there we steered north a little bit in order to get a better view of the revered Rockbridge Baths. Lauded by Robert E. Lee, the noted French artist and world traveler, Pierre Daura, captured with canvas and brush the scenic beauty of Rockbridge County, and endeared its rustic New World nature to millions of Europeans before the Second World War.

"Larry, I'm getting hungry; how about a sandwich?" I asked my friend.

We enjoyed our breakfast of ham and cheese sandwiches and cold milk as we relaxed above the diminutive village of Raphine. Taken from the Greek word, "raphis," which means "to sew," the name "Raphine" was chosen for the town shortly before the Civil War in order to honor Mr. James Gibbs, a local farmer and inventor. Whether it elicited joy or consternation from his wife has been forgotten, but he patented the first chain stitch, single thread sewing machine in June of 1857. The McCormick family farm is also nearby. Cyrus McCormick was the inventor of the first mechanical reaper in 1831.

Looking out ahead, down the spectacular Shenandoah Valley, named after an Indian expression meaning "Beautiful Daughter of the Stars," we followed the "Great Wagon Road" to Staunton. It is the birthplace of President Woodrow Wilson, as well as the iconic Country Music group, The Statler Brothers. The idyllic community of Bridgewater slipped by on our left. Nestled along the North River, Bridgewater is the home of the aptly named Bridgewater College.

We flew in silence for several minutes – taking in the awesomeness of the valley below. It dawned on me that a person would not be able to travel more than a mile in any direction from any point in the Shenandoah Valley without coming upon something imbued with historical magnificence. I also thought of the abundant decorative kiosks tucked away along the back roads of the valley stocked to their ceilings with fresh apple cider and homemade apple butter. I had never tasted any better.

"Hey, Dayeve, how ya'll doin' back there?" Steve radioed. "Gettin' hungry again. We're on your tail." I radioed back.

At that point Steve said he wanted us to move up alongside his airplane so Jim could get some aerial photos of us. Larry and I moved into a line abreast position off to their right for a few moments, and then we bobbed up and down so they could take some good shots of a clean and polished Cessna 172 in flight. It was thrilling to be that close to another airplane, but I didn't like the idea of staying long in such close proximity without more thorough training in formation flying. So we soon moved back to our safe position – behind and to the right.

"We're getting close to Harrisonburg. Debbie said she graduated from James Madison two years ago. She was a music major." Steve informed us.

"Well, ask her to serenade us while we're being mesmerized by natural beauty." I said.

After a brief pause he chuckled, "She said she couldn't even sing in the shower this early."

Harrisonburg, named for the English settler Thomas Harrison, who built his family's home among several natural springs in the area, was also the home of James Madison University. Founded as a women's college in 1908, The State Normal and Industrial School For Women, the name was changed to James Madison University in 1924, honoring the fourth president of the United States. Harrisonburg is also noted for harboring the first known town council in America that attempted to fill its coffers through a tax on dogs in about 1852. Whether the ordinance originally stated "dog ownership," as in the number of dogs a person had residing on his property, or a weight-based tax was pure speculation. Reportedly, the measure was buried by the citizens in court. In either case, the council members were greeted on the streets for months afterward by barks and bays from the more vocal constituents – not to mention the four-legged ones….

We continued our formation northeastward past New Market battlefield. New Market is a small agrarian village about forty- five miles southwest of Winchester, Virginia. General John Sevier, a revolutionary patriot and state representative from North Carolina, founded the town in the late 1770s. New Market's claim to fame, however, is the historic Battle of New Market, fought in May of 1864.

The historian author, Burke Davis, described the event in his book "The Civil War, Strange and Fascinating Facts."

"The most celebrated schoolboy performance of the war was the baptism of fire of the Virginia Military Institute Cadet Corps at the Battle of New Market, Virginia – the only such instance in the war. The action took place in the Shenandoah Valley outside the village of New Market, in rolling hill country between a fork of the Shenandoah river and the flank of Massanutten Mountain. It was fought on May 15, 1864, between a Federal force of some 6,500 under General Franz Sigel and the confederates about 4,500 strong, under General John C. Breckinridge.

The Cadets had marched in from Lexington, leaving the younger ones on their campus disconsolate, feeling disgraced at missing the opportunity to fight. The Corps was 215 strong when it reached New Market, and was put into the opening battle on Sunday morning. All the Cadets were eighteen or younger, some of them sixteen, and reputedly even younger. (Tradition has it that some were only fourteen.)

They marched behind their commander, Lieutenant Colonel Scott Shipp, twenty-four, who rode a dappled gray horse. The boy soldiers heard their first cheering near the front, as General Breckinridge rode by "like the Cid," in the words of young John Wise, son of a Virginia governor. Boys in the artillery battery recognized friends among the Cadets as they passed, and called gibes:

'Here come the wagon dogs! Ho, bombproofs, get outa them good clothes!'

Some of the Cadets wanted to fight for their honor on the spot, but were headed on. John Wise and three others were left behind as baggage guards, but he made a dramatic speech to his crew and they deserted the post, leaving a Negro driver in charge of the wagon; they joined the Cadet column.

Henry Wise, another of the Governor's sons, was one of their Captains; the night before he had chided the boys for cursing, and for chicken stealing, but had later eaten some of the cold fowl in camp with them.

About noon, when a black thundercloud hung over the valley, the Cadets joined the confederate line of battle in the center – the place of honor, the history conscious among them thought. They came to a hillcrest, passed their own small battery in action, and went down a slope into the open. They heard musket fire and artillery, but nothing seemed close until a clap burst overhead. Five of the boys in C company went down: Captain Govan Hill, Merritt, Read, Woodlief, and John Wise. Just before he lost consciousness Wise saw Sergeant Cabell look at him with a pitying expression.

"Close up, men," Cabell ordered.

The line reached a ravine within 300 yards of a busy Federal battery – the six fine guns of the 30th New York, under Captain Albert von Kleiser. The ravine gave cover from the cannon, which fired from crest studded with young cedars. The ditch was filled with cedar scrub, briers, stones, and stumps, and the Cadets were a few minutes in passing through; even so, they were out before the older veterans on their flank, the 62nd Virginia.

Once, the Cadets halted under heavy fire while the file straightened, and the advanced flanks came even with the center. A dwelling, the Bushong house, split their line, and by companies they passed on either side, marking time beyond, restoring the line once more.

Colonel Shipp halted them and shouted, "Fix bayonets!" Almost immediately he was struck by a shell fragment, and fell. Several Cadets were wounded at this moment, and the file lay down. Someone yelled an order to fall back on the next Confederate unit, but Cadet Pizzini of B Company swore and said he would shoot the first man who moved backward.

Captain Henry Wise jumped to his feet and shouted for a charge on the Federal guns, and the line went up after him.

A Federal Signal Corps Captain, Franklin E. Town, on the hill beside Von Kleiser's battery, watched the Cadets come on with such fascination that it did not occur to him that he might be captured. The big guns had already changed from shrapnel to canister and then double canister, so that the air was filled with murderous small iron balls. The Cadet Corps did not falter, and in these last yards lost most of its dead and wounded. Captain Town wrote:

'They came on steadily up the slope. Their advance was fierce. Their line was as perfectly preserved as if on dress parade. They would reach us without pause. Our gunners loaded at the last without stopping to sponge, and I think it would have been impossible to eject from six guns more missiles than these boys faced in their wild charge up that hill.'

The Cadets were soon among the Federal gunners with bayonets flashing. Lieutenant Hanna felled one young soldier with a plunge through the middle with his dress sword, and Winder Garrett caught another through the heart with his bayonet. One Cadet found Lieutenant Colonel W.S. Lincoln of the 34th Massachusetts on the ground, pinned by his fallen horse, but still defiant, and ready to shoot with a cocked pistol; the Cadet ran him through the chest with his bayonet.

With wild yells the Cadets greeted the sight of the Institute flag over the bloodied hilltop, waved by their tall ensign, Evans, and celebrated their victory over the Union gunners while the rainstorm broke. Of John Wise's disobedient baggage guard of four, one was dead and two were wounded. The Corps had eight dead and forty-four wounded, all told.

The 62nd Virginia, charging beside them, had seven of its ten Captains shot down, four dead, and a total of 241 killed and wounded.

The chase went on for three miles as Sigel's force withdrew to Rude's Hill and beyond, and there was fighting, especially by artillery, until well after dark.

The next day, when he passed the VMI battery at the roadside, General Breckinridge stopped to pass compliments:

"Boys, the work you did yesterday will make you famous." Dave Pierce, a boy soldier not too young to understand military life, called back: "Fame's all right, General, but for God's sake where's your commissary wagon?"

An impressive ceremony still a part of VMI life today celebrates May 15th on the Lexington campus. Selected cadets at roll call snap their replies as the names of the New Market casualties are called: "Dead on the field of honor, sir."

—————◆◆◆◆◆—————

As our two modern aircraft winged gracefully over the silent battlefield at New Market I felt amazed at the thought of how much life had changed in the country in less than 110 years – just over one average man's lifetime. I was the same age as most of the cadets who fought on those grounds that venerated day in 1864.

Just a few miles up the valley from New Market we passed the historic town of Mount Jackson.

"Hey, Dave! There's the old covered bridge down there at Mount Jackson." Larry chimed.

I banked the airplane to the right in order to get a better look at the structure. The abundant foliage concealed each entrance to the bridge, but the span was clearly visible. Its rustic appearance blended artfully with the fall colors surrounding it.

"Steve, let's drop down and do a low pass over the covered bridge so Larry can take some pictures." I called over the radio.

I followed Steve's airplane in a wide descending arc to the left. We went all the way around and re-intercepted the north fork of the Shenandoah River about a mile west of the bridge at about seven hundred feet above the ground. As we approached the old bridge we all had our cameras ready to shoot.

The Meems Bottom Covered Bridge was completed in 1893 by Mr. Franklin Wissler in order to facilitate the access to his apple orchards and the Strathmore Farm, located on the east side of the Shenandoah River's north fork. Its wooden 'Burr Arch' stretches almost 180 feet. Donated to the state highway department in the 1930s in exchange for its upkeep and maintenance, it has since been placed on the National Historic Register.

Originally founded as the town of Mount Pleasant in 1812, the General Assembly of Virginia changed the name to Mount Jackson in 1826, in order to honor President Andrew Jackson, who was a frequent visitor. General "Stonewall" Jackson established his headquarters in the Rude house, built on Rude's Hill, just south of town, in 1862. It was the same house where President Andrew Jackson used to stay while visiting Mount Pleasant.

Satisfied with our photography of the bridge, we continued northeast toward our destination, Harpers Ferry. We passed Woodstock, where in 1776, the reverend John

Peter Gabriel Muhlenburg, originally from Pennsylvania, gave his rousing final sermon before stepping back to toss away his clerical robe revealing a dashing Continental Army Officer's uniform. Before marching out the door his final words were: "There is a time for praying and a time for fighting. The time for fighting has come." He went on to distinguish himself in many battles during the War for Independence.

We dropped down to a low altitude as we flew across the famous "Seven Bends" of the Shenandoah River. It was a mystery to me how such an ancient river could maintain so many 180-degree turns in so short a distance without altering its channels. With the bright sky reflecting off the water, it looked as if some giant being had been toying with a bottle of Elmer's Glue as he poured in a continuous wave pattern across his worksheet.

Strasburg was next up the line. Its first inhabitants were mostly of German origin. In fact, in 1761, when the town was founded, it would have been difficult to find anyone who spoke fluent English in Strasburg. Being the tip of the spear for the Confederate States in 1861, Strasburg bore the brunt of the fighting in the Shenandoah Valley during the Civil War. It changed sides many times as armies came marching through. The cognitive reasoning of the Germanic peoples in the lower Shenandoah Valley has been said to be behind the common understanding that "going down" the valley actually means heading northeast, generally thought of as "up." Conversely, "going up" the valley, means heading southwest. It all has to do with altitude, not direction.

Steve called about that time.

"Dave, I'm going to fly a heading of about zero–six–zero degrees. That should put us on a good intercept course to Harpers Ferry. We should be able to see the Shenandoah River where it widens south of Charles Town before we get there. The next big town we see will be Winchester. How does that look to you?"

I didn't want to tell Steve that I had already put my map away, and I had no idea if a zero–six–zero degree heading was right or not. But, I knew that if we simply followed the Shenandoah River we'd eventually fly right over the town of Harpers Ferry.

Our fuel gauges were showing more than enough gas to turn around and fly all the way back to Roanoke. We'd only been in the air about one hour and ten minutes, so we had plenty of gas. I dialed in the 042-degree radial of the Linden VOR. The 060-degree heading would put us on an intercept course of that radial at about fifteen miles south of our destination.

"We're almost there, Larry." I chimed.

"Good. I'm ready to get out and walk some." He said.

We motored together another twenty-five miles, past Winchester and Berryville, admiring the beautiful fall morning with its spectacular scenery beneath us. Finally, about thirteen minutes later, the VOR needle began inching towards center from its full right deflection.

"Is your needle coming in, Steve?" I asked him over the radio.

"Yeah, it just jumped off the peg. You want to start down?" He asked.

"I'm behind you. We go where you go."

The Shenandoah River widened ahead as it began to undulate back and forth just across the border of West Virginia – like it was not quite sure where it was supposed to go next.

"There's the border." Steve called.

"We'll be over Harpers Ferry in seven minutes." I radioed back.

We continued our slow descent from three thousand five hundred feet, following the meandering ancient river. The airstrip we were looking for, set in a narrow valley one ridge over to the west from the Shenandoah River, was south of Route 340 and east of Halltown, W.V. We were to look for a drive-in movie theater at the intersection of routes 340 and 27. Following the meandering blacktop road south from the drive-in, we would soon spot the airfield, aligned generally north and south along the base of Schoolhouse Ridge. A long narrow shipping canal had been dug paralleling the road that led down to Millville. It probably served as a logging canal at one time.

Spying the town dead ahead, Steve radioed. "There's Harpers Ferry. I'm gonna turn left a little bit to find Halltown, then the drive-in."

"Roger that." I replied.

In just under two minutes Steve and I spotted the airstrip at about the same time.

"There's the landing strip, Larry." I said.

Surveying the field from above, it appeared to be smooth and well kept. A windsock was located at about the middle of the strip – close to the road. As we circled the field we could see the yellow sock hanging limp, indicating no wind to speak of. A Piper aircraft and two automobiles were parked along the eastern edge of the runway. Steve and I had already determined that under a no-wind condition we would land to the north, as the field was higher on the north end than the south. I circled the farm again as Steve started his approach.

"Looks like somebody's waiting for us down there, Steve." I called.

"Yeah, I hope they're friendly." He replied sarcastically.

Larry and I watched Steve land and taxi to the edge, and then we began our approach to the field. As we descended over the blazoned tree line on the south end, I could see that the deep green grass had been recently mowed. It could have easily passed for a well-designed golf course. It was any pilot's perfect grass runway – just what we had imagined.

The wheels of the Cessna slid onto the turf ever so softly, and we rolled to a slow taxi speed without the need for breaking at all. I pulled up next to Steve's airplane and shut down. We were excited to be in Harpers Ferry, thrilled by the beauty and the history we had witnessed during the last hour and a half, satisfied by the precise landing I had just executed on a picture- perfect grass airfield, and more than ready to find a men's room.

Chapter Eighteen

The Great Awakening

"The passage of the Patowmac through the Blue Ridge is perhaps one of the most stupendous scenes in nature. You stand on a very high point of land, looking toward the rising sun. On your right comes up the Shenandoah, having ranged along the foot of the mountain a hundred miles to seek a vent. On your left, also in search of passage, approaches the Patowmac. In the moment of their junction they rush together against the mountain, rend it asunder and pass off to the sea. The first glance of this scene hurries our senses into the opinion that this earth has been created in time, that the mountains were formed first, the rivers began to flow afterwards, that in this place particularly they have been so dammed up by the Blue Ridge of mountains as to have formed an ocean which filled the whole valley; that, continuing to rise, they have at last broken over this spot and have torn the mountain down from its summit to its base. The piles of rock on each hand, but particularly on the

*Shenandoah, the evident marks of their disruptions
and avulsions from their beds by the most powerful
agents in nature, corroborate the impression. But
the distant finishing, which nature has given the
picture, is of a very different character. It is a true
contrast to the former. The distant is as placid and
delightful as the near is wild and tremendous. For
the mountains being cloven asunder, she presents to
your eye, through the cleft, a small catch of smooth
blue horizon, at an infinite distance in that the
plain country, inviting you, as it were, from the
riot and tumult roaring around to pass through the
breach and participate in the calm below. Here the
eye ultimately composes itself; and that way, too,
the road happens to actually lead. You cross the
Patowmac above the junction, pass along its side
through the base of the mountain for three miles, the
terrible precipice hanging in fragments above you,
and within about twenty miles reach Fredericktown
and the fine country beyond. This scene alone is
worth a voyage across the Atlantic."*

Thomas Jefferson, 1785

All of us were more than ready for a hearty breakfast as
the hostess seated us on the shaded veranda overlooking
the Potomac River. (*Po-to'-mac, Indian, "The place where
people trade."*) There were now seven members in the group.
Jim's dad and uncle met us at the field and drove us the
short distance into Harpers Ferry to the world class Hilltop
House. The elegant hotel, built in 1888, had been the
opulent harborage of past dignitaries such as Mark Twain,

Pearl S. Buck, Carl Sandburg, as well as numerous U.S. presidents. The hotel's tranquil ambience seemed to beckon long ago memories into vivid reality. Gazing down at the turbulent waters that defined the confluence of the two rivers, I could almost see the Union gunboats churning white water as they fought their way upstream towards the town.

Jim's father, Daniel Ewing, was a history teacher at a local high school in the area. He was working on his doctorate in early American history; his goal was a professorship at James Madison University. Mr. Ewing was of average height, perhaps 5'10", but his penetrating brown eyes and untimorous manner gave me the impression of a much taller man. When he spoke he did so with authority and confidence. From his son Jim he had learned of the reason for our visit, and he could not resist the urge to tutor us all on the subject of John Brown and Harpers Ferry. I was delighted. So as we enjoyed our breakfast we came to know Daniel and his brother, Peter, and also the story of a convicted and unalterable soul.

"Well, David, Jim tells me you guys are using this trip to Harpers Ferry as an excuse to spend your money on flying." Mr. Ewing finally broke the ice.

"I prefer to think of it as a strategic manipulation of available resources to expand our knowledge of American history, Mr. Ewing." I replied jokingly as I set my tape recorder on the table.

After pausing only briefly, he responded with raised eyebrows. "Have you considered politics as a career?"

He then began to expostulate on the enigmatic figure, John Brown:

"To understand, if only academically, the man John Brown, you have to start with the religion of the Puritans. Within the Church of England during the 16th century, there were people who collectively thought that the English Reformation had not gone nearly far enough to purge every drop of Catholic influence from the doctrine and structure of the Anglican Church. They wanted further purification. Their aim was to eliminate every ounce of influence the Catholic Church had over the population of England. Most of these people were followers of John Calvin. Calvin was educated as a lawyer in the 1500's, but he came to preach the Bible, because that's what he believed he was called by God to do. I'm not going to get into a religious discussion here, but I will say his views differed with the Catholic Church mainly on the topics of God's sovereignty and the salvation of mankind. As you research this, you'll come upon the argument of works vs. gifts. But that's a whole library in itself.

"Anyway, this group, these Puritans, became dissatisfied with the course of religiosity in England, and they set out to emigrate to the new world during the whole of the 1600's. The Puritans believed in a direct, personal relationship with God, a sincere personal moral conduct, and very simple church and worship services – as opposed to the opulence of the Catholic Church and its reverence for a single man known as the Pope. To put it another way, they believed in walking the walk, not just talking the talk. In their eyes, if you believe something, you should live like you believe it. They despised the authority that the Pope and the Bishops held over the common man. They believed only in the truth of the Bible – not the words of a greedy authoritarian.

"A major player during this time of reformation in England as the Puritan movement was taking hold, was a quasi-nobleman by the name of Oliver Cromwell. You'll have to do some research on him, because John Brown was heavily influenced by his tactics and beliefs. For instance: One of Cromwell's long-standing orders in and after battle, was for his armies not to harm civilians - and even combatants if they had put down their swords. As long as the enemy held arms there would be no quarter taken. Everyone was to be eliminated. And believe me, the blood flowed copiously. Thousands upon thousands were killed during the reformation. Cromwell was as ruthless as they come as a military commander. But, he was also a Puritan, and his convictions as a Puritan forbade him to harm those who were at his mercy. John Brown upheld these same convictions his whole life. Even his military tactics mimicked those of Cromwell. He was not afraid to shed unrighteous blood.

"In the whole of English history, I would say that there is only one man who could best Oliver Cromwell for notoriety, and that would be Winston Churchill. A word of caution here: Let me tell you straight out. If you ever travel to Ireland, or even Scotland, don't mention the name of Oliver Cromwell. You might not escape with a whole neck.

At this point, my traveling companions excused themselves in order to hike down the botanical trail from the hotel to the Potomac River. They said they would meet up with us somewhere in the town down below after my discussion with Mr. Ewing. I then returned my attention to my personal tutor for the day.

"Oliver Cromwell essentially led the revolt in England by the Parliamentarians and their New Model Army against the monarchy and its Loyalists during the English Revolution in the 1640s. It could be said that this was England's great awakening. Everyone who despised the theocratic rule of the Catholic Church heralded the revolution. After King Charles the First was executed in 1649, the victorious Parliamentarians formed what came to be known as the Commonwealth of England. Cromwell led this government in one form or another until his death in 1658. His title became "Lord Protectorate."

"The focal point of all of this war and fighting was centered in the Bible. And, more precisely, was Jesus Christ himself. One of my favorite quotes in the Bible is found in the book of Luke, chapter twelve. Verses forty-nine through fifty-three quote Jesus as saying he has come to bring strife and division to the world, to nations, to families. As a teacher of secular history, I feel like I'm in the grandstands watching this very parade of tender box passions roll past before my eyes. And the participants don't even realize they're in a parade at all.

"It is interesting to note, paralleling his Biblical beliefs, Cromwell also invited the Jews to return to England in 1657, after noting that the Dutch economy had improved vastly with their direct participation in Dutch economic affairs. That makes you think a little, doesn't it? King Edward the First had stupidly expelled all Jews from England some 350 years earlier. Makes you wonder about the mental capabilities of the Nazis and the Iranians, huh?

"Now, what is important about all this? The religious convictions of Oliver Cromwell, along with his stoic character, had a direct impact on the Puritans of the time and their descendants. John Brown was not only a Puritan, his father's blood descended directly from Puritans who escaped persecution in England in 1620. In fact, a direct descendant of John Brown was a Pilgrim. A *Pilgrim* is defined as someone who travels, or someone who travels for religious reasons. That's all it means. Anyway, this individual landed at Plymouth Rock after crossing the Atlantic on the Mayflower. I think it was his great, great, great grandfather on his father's side. And these Puritanical beliefs dominated New England for generations. So, you see, this unyielding, tough-as-nails character trait that seemed to define the average Puritan was seeded into John Brown when he entered the world in the spring of 1800 at Torrington, Connecticut."

The waitress interrupted the discourse when she approached the table to inquire about our needs, and it gave me a chance to ask Mr. Ewing a question that had been on my mind:

"Mr. Ewing, my father often says that most wars have been fought in the name of religion. Would you agree with that statement in general?"

He thought deeply for a moment, and then he answered.

"Many have. Some have not. Of course, the Bible is full of spiritual conflict – both figuratively and literally. Many wars have begun through a misguided sense of nationalistic pride. World War I is a prime example of nationalism run amok. One of the definitions of Nationalism is the policy of promoting or advocating the interests of one's own country irrespective of the needs or desires of other countries. Simply speaking, it's selfishness. I want what I want, and I don't care what you want or need. An attitude like that could be said to have its derivations in a lack of spirituality or religion. The true believers and followers of the teachings of Christ do not suffer from a crippling plague like nationalistic pride. Pride in one's country is an admirable trait, but true Nationalism is something else all together.

"Now, on the other hand, many wars have begun through a misguided sense of religiosity. Look at the crusades for example. Most people think the crusaders were Christians attempting to eliminate all Islamic influence in the Holy Land. You'll have to dive deeply into all this if you want to uncover the specifics, but I will tell you that the Catholic Church – not because of any loyalty to Christ, waged the Crusades against the Muslims because of the greed and the lust for power and wealth. That's a bold statement that I will simply let lay there by itself.

"The absolutely most pivotal imbroglio, if you will, we face today, is the conflict waging between the Jews and the Arabs; more specifically, the Israelis and the Palestinians. There's a war on right now – as you probably know. And I believe things will only get worse as the decades roll by. The world will someday be consumed by the antipathy between the followers of Allah and the believers of Jehovah.

"Most people in the world believe there is only one God. He is the creator of all things. But Allah and Jehovah are not the same. They are said to have totally different character traits. One is knowable; the other is not. Both are mysterious and unfathomable. But, one seeks an affinity with mankind. The Bible says He came to the earth Himself, in physical form, in order to teach us about Himself. This GOD gives evidence of his graciousness and a way to approach Him personally. The other god is aloof and indifferent. He does not seek friendship with man. He chooses who, and who will not be his subjects at whim. There is no way for man to understand his heart, his personality. And there is no evidence that he ever existed, except in the mind of one man. And it was his wife who pushed him into spreading that belief. He thought he was insane.

"Dave, the world is not big enough for two Gods. One of them will someday be proven false – a figment of one's imagination, a stumbling block to the truth - the true God. Which one will it be?

"To answer your question, yes. Most wars have been fought, from one viewpoint or another, because of some religious aspect. John Brown's war against slavery in the 1850s was certainly no exception."

We finished our working breakfast and decided to explore the sights in Harpers Ferry. As we descended stone-paved Potomac Street towards the center of town, Mr. Ewing pointed ahead to a diminutive white brick building that looked like a one room country school with oversized windows.

"That's John Brown's fort where he sought refuge during his siege of the armory during his raid on October 16th, 1859. It used to be over here, on the left." He said, as he pointed toward the opposite side of the cobbled street.

"The National Park Service restored it in 1968. After the raid the building spent time in Chicago during the World's Columbian Exposition in 1891. So it's been around. Of course, during the raid it was actually a fire-engine house.

"So Dave, let's approach this subject with a reporter's perspective. Who was John Brown? What did he do that was so worthy of investigation? When did it happen? What was going on in the country at that time? Why did he do what he did? What was the result of his actions? What does history say about it all, and how has it affected us today? I'll attempt to answer these questions one-at-a-time."

We arrived after a few steps at Ground Zero for John Brown. The quaint little engine house had been completely restored to look as it did in 1859 – complete with a period fire engine.

"John Brown and his small band of dedicated followers, including five freed slaves, launched their raid on the Federal arsenal here in order to capture weapons and ammunition to distribute to slaves across Virginia. John hoped to incite a huge slave revolt that would spread across the South like wildfire. Although, in actuality, he knew that in order to be successful he would have to command a series of lightning-fast, hit-and-run raids on plantations in Virginia for weeks before his army would be strong enough to wage a full-scale war against the Southern Militias.

"After the initial assault, he took many hostages - thirty or more - and sought refuge in this building with eleven of them while he waited for his deployed men to bring freed slaves into Harpers Ferry so they could join the insurrection and take arms. Unfortunately, it didn't work out that way.

"Most of the Negro slaves were too afraid to leave their homes. They simply couldn't believe white men would come onto their masters' farms in the middle of the night and attempt to entice them to revolt. As it happened, instead of cutting his losses and heading for the mountains like he had originally planned, John tarried a bit too long in the engine house here, and soon found himself surrounded by an angry mob of towns' folk and local farmers. And it turned into a drunken rabble. Shots were fired, and several people on both sides were killed and wounded, including two of Brown's older sons, Oliver and Watson. Brown and his men held off hundreds of militiamen from around the area for three days until the Union contingent, under the command of Robert E. Lee, arrived from Washington to charge in and settle the matter. And that's exactly what happened.

"Brown's small force was overwhelmed by a full-frontal assault by a force of ninety bloodthirsty Marines. Lee was a Colonel in the Union Army at that time – before the Civil War. They call that the "Antebellum" period – "before the war." Anyway, the hostages he had taken were rescued, and John Brown himself was wounded severely, and captured. All of his men in the engine house were either killed or captured with him. The only reason John was not killed then was because the young officer who slashed at him with his sword had mistakenly sheathed his parade dress sword before leaving Washington instead of his battle saber. So the wounds Brown suffered by that sword were almost superficial.

"As I said before, John Brown was a Puritan, and he held strict Puritanical beliefs. To him slavery was an abomination. But, John Brown was more. He was an abolitionist. He was a farmer. He was a businessman, although not a very good one; he was often too honest to make it in the businesses he tried. He was the father of many children – by two wives. His first wife, Dianthe, died shortly after giving birth to their sixth child - a boy, who also died almost immediately. His second wife, Mary Day, outlived him by a number of years in a community he helped found called North Elba, New York, up in the Adirondack Mountains. Incidentally, "Adirondack" comes from an old Indian word that means "They eat trees." I think they were speaking of some other tribe. Anyway, North Elba is where John Brown was buried after being tried, convicted, and hung in Charles Town, Virginia. You guys probably flew past Charles Town, West Virginia on the way here. North Elba was a farming community for runaway slaves whom John Brown helped to escape slavery in the south via the Underground Railroad."

I could easily tell that Mr. Ewing was quite passionate about his history. The more he lectured, the more peppery his words became. His eyes were burning with brightness, and his hands stabbed with overt flagrance. He continued with gusto.

"Now, John Brown didn't simply build a town for escaped Negroes. He built his family's home there among them. He lived with them. He had them in his home. He treated them as equals in every way. Back in 1850, conduct like that from a white man was unheard of. You simply did not keep the company of blacks in that day. It was *anathema*, as the Catholics like to say. You, as a white man, could get yourself hung if you associated with slaves, or even free blacks – especially in the south. But John Brown was his own man; he was an egalitarian.

"John Brown had come to hate slavery as a young boy growing up in Ohio. His father was an avid abolitionist, and also hated slavery. His Puritan upbringing taught him that everyone was created equally. And that, to him, meant all races, colors, and creeds. The Constitution said so. The Bible said so. And the Browns remained Old-Style Puritans their entire lives. They held on to their beliefs even after many others allowed syncretism to gradually dilute their beliefs. The Hebrews fell into the syncretism trap after they invaded the Promised Land. They began to accept the false gods, the beliefs, the traditions, and the customs of other peoples. And where did it take them? To Babylon, into captivity. And that's not just Biblical history. That's ancient secular history. And the parade rolls on…."

As I explored the engine house, along with its period artifacts, I listened carefully to the learned words of a man that had obviously educated himself in historical facts and anecdotes. I tried to picture the scene as it must have looked in October of 1859….

"John Brown had two important revelations in his life that came to him as a boy. One was an engraved repulsion of the military. He vowed never to serve in the Army because of many vile things he heard and witnessed from soldiers against Indians and Negroes – and those who were weaker. The other was his hatred toward slavery and his vow to destroy it any way he could.

"One day, while lodging with some relatives during a trek across Ohio and Pennsylvania when he was about twelve years old, he befriended a young negro slave boy about his own age. John wrote that the slave boy was intelligent and benevolent towards him. He saw that he was eager to learn of the world, and he could hold his own in any game of wits. The father of the house heaped praise after praise on young John for being brave enough to travel so far from home without his parents. The man showered John with compliments and gifts. But, at the same time, the man relentlessly beat the young slave boy with any household tool he could get his hands on – even to the point of severe injury and blood. John was fed very well. But the slave boy was thrown scraps from the table. John slept in a warm bed close to a fireplace. The slave boy slept outdoors in the cold under the porch in filthy rags with no bedding whatsoever. John would soon return to his home and family. The slave boy had no mother or father to yearn for. He would be forever homeless, forever hopeless. It was then that John Brown swore a seething allegiance to the destruction of slavery. He would commit his entire life to it. Inevitably, he would give his life for it.

"So you see? John Brown was not a madman. He was consciously convicted by virtue and physically committed by circumstance. If he had not been such a stalwart Christian man, totally given to the teachings of Christ, he probably would have faltered and fallen away from what he believed was his commission by God. But John Brown knew the Bible as well as any preacher of his day – in fact, better than most.

"I want to read you a couple of things here." Mr. Ewing continued as he reached for the portfolio he had brought with him. "The first one is a portion of John Brown's address to the court during his trial in Charles Town."

He handed me the paper, and I began to read aloud John Brown's own words as he faced imminent death:

> *"'...I wish to say, furthermore, that you had better – all you people in the South, prepare yourselves for a settlement of the question that must come up sooner than you are prepared for it. The sooner you are prepared, the better. You may dispose of me very easily; I am nearly disposed of now; but this question, this Negro question is still to be settled. The end of that is not yet.'"*

Mr. Ewing then handed me another one and said,

"The next thing I have for you here are two excerpts from the last letter John Brown wrote to his family in up-state New York before his execution on December 2, 1859."

> "'...I am waiting the hour of my public murder with great composure of mind and cheerfulness, feeling the strong assurance that in no other possible way could I be used to so much advantage to the cause of good and of humanity, and that nothing that either I or all of my family have sacrificed or suffered will be lost...'"

A little further into the letter he wrote a personal note to his children:

> "'...My dear younger children, will you listen to this last poor admonition of one who can only love you? Oh! Be determined at once to give your whole heart to God, and let nothing shake, nor alter that resolution. You need have no fears of regretting it. Do not be vain and thoughtless, but sober minded; and let me entreat you all to love the whole remnant of our once great family. Try to build up again your broken walls, and to make the utmost of every stone that is left. Nothing can so tend to make life a blessing as the consciousness

that your life and example bless and leave you the stronger. Still, it is ground of the utmost comfort to my mind to know that so many of you as have had the opportunity have given some proof of your fidelity to the great family of men. Be faithful unto death. From the exercise of habitual love to mankind it cannot be very difficult to learn to love his Maker."'

We stood silently for several moments letting John Brown's own words echo off the storied walls of the engine house where he made his stand. Then my teacher brought the lesson into a more personal perspective for me.

"Think about that for a moment, Dave. Just let it sink in. How many people have you known who have been so courageous, so dedicated? Think of a flagpole standing in a gale force wind during a driving rain. Picture it as nighttime. It's completely dark. The howling wind is deafening. Suddenly the night is electrified by a bolt of lightning. For one second it's as bright as day. You look toward that flagpole, and there it is, your flag. Your banner, which stands for everything you believe in, is standing tall and strong. It's being whipped and pummeled by the elements; however, it is undaunted – solid as a rock. That flagpole is John Brown. He stood up for morality and righteousness – even when the law of the land forbade him in his actions and beliefs. And he stood alone, which is so often the case.

"He knew he had the power of God on his side, and he believed God would use him to accomplish the task of ridding the country of the scourge of slavery. No one else in the entire country believed in the cause as strongly as he did. Even the northern abolitionists – preachers, writers, college professors, and conductors on the Underground Railroad - were weak in John's eyes. They believed in the cause, abolition, but they were not ready to risk their necks for it. And most of them didn't even come close to believing the Negroes were in any way equal to the white man. Even Abraham Lincoln didn't believe that – as much as he hated slavery. But John Brown believed the Negro, in every way, to be equal with whites. And, what's more important than believing it is living it. And that is why I admire the man like I do.

"It wasn't so much the cause he died for that impresses me – righteous as that cause was. It was the creed of the man himself - the courage to stand up for right – even when no one will stand with you. Frankly, I have to ask myself if I would be able to follow my heart to such lengths. Would I be willing to fight to the death for a cause that I believed was morally right? I don't know. Would I be willing to pick up a gun and fight my fellow countrymen in order to preserve the Constitution of our founding fathers when the current civil law, the legal system tells me that I do not have that right? Could I, with a sound mind and spirit, actually fight against my own police and justice system if I was convinced that I was right by the Bible and the Constitution? I just don't know. But, you know, Dave, one day in this very country of ours it may come down to that.

"Through our own ineptitude, indolence, and apathy, we may one day find ourselves governed by Americans who would forfeit everything the Constitution stands for. We may be faced with the inevitable outcome of losing every freedom we ever had – all in the name of safety, security, or fairness. We lose more freedoms every year already. The liberal judges are sneaking their way onto law benches around the country every year. And most of us don't even notice. When that day of reckoning comes, we may have no alternative but armed insurrection. On that day, if it ever comes, America will experience its own great awakening."

Mr. Ewing's words hung heavily in the air for several moments like an enshrouding fog. As I studied the tranquil little fire-engine house I was struck with the sobering thought of knowing that the course of the entire country was altered within its nescient brick walls so long ago. The shockwave of one single event in 1859 was still being felt across the land on that beautiful autumn day in 1973. As we turned away to continue our tour of the town, Mr. Ewing said with a smile,

"Isn't history a wonderful teacher?"

———◆•◆••◆———

The shadows had grown much shorter by the time we met up with the rest of the group at the bookshop on Shenandoah Street. Larry had parked himself on a wooden bench under the awning outside the door with a cool drink and was watching the visitors stroll by on this gorgeous fall midday. I found Steve and Jim inside gazing through a large volume about trains. They were particularly interested in the railroad history of Harpers Ferry. The B&O Railroad (Baltimore & Ohio), one of the four railroads on the board game Monopoly (and by the way, the only one of the four that did not serve Atlantic City, N.J.), laid its main line through

Harpers Ferry on its way west to the frontier country. George Washington had actually done some surveying for that route many years before. The other railroad serving Harpers Ferry at the time was the Winchester & Potomac. It ran south along the Shenandoah River out of Harpers Ferry. The little town served as a major interchange of merchandise before, during, and after the Civil War.

We found Debbie and Peter browsing through the gift area where Mr. Ewing helped me select several books. Each would guide me skillfully on an informational journey through history about John Brown. I read about his raid on the armory there in 1859, and how it culminated several decades of his personal struggle with slavery in America. I found books that corroborated Mr. Ewing's stories about the effective beginnings of armed combat in the Kansas territory (in which John Brown played a pivotal role), before the official start of the Civil War in South Carolina.

Most importantly, I discovered how critical John Brown's actions were to the entire nation before the war. In effect, he galvanized both sides against each other. His spirit in death emboldened the northern abolitionists. Through the works of Transcendentalist authors such as Henry David Thoreau and Ralph Waldo Emerson, who lionized John Brown, the unlawful but moral efforts in the Underground Railroad were greatly expanded. John Brown's death boiled a cauldron of paranoia in the South – mostly through the printing of sensationalistic newspaper articles and ignitable editorials about the Republican Party's culpability in the raid on Harpers Ferry. These fears only hastened the South's withdrawal from the Union. John Brown was a martyr for the Northern cause; he was the South's most fearsome nemesis. Victor Hugo, a leading European literary writer of the period, wrote from the island of Guernsey on the day of John Brown's execution:

> "At the thought of the United States of America, a majestic form rises in the mind. Washington. In this country of Washington what is now taking place? John Brown, condemned to death, is to be hanged today. His hangman is not the attorney Hunter, nor the judge Parker, nor Governor Wise, nor the little State of Virginia. His hangman, we shudder to say it, is the whole American Republic. Politically speaking, the murder of John Brown will be an irrevocable mistake. It will deal the union a concealed wound, which will finally sunder the states. Let America know and consider that there is only one thing more shocking than Cain killing Abel, it is Washington killing Spartacus."

John Brown went to his death knowing exactly what his execution would bring about – the end of slavery in America. And to that end, it is no surprise to learn that Union soldiers marched into southern cities singing the battle hymn that echoed for decades across southern farms and plantations like the roar of a ravenous lion: John Brown's Body.

"John Brown's body lies a-moldering in the grave; (3x) His soul is marching on.

(Chorus)
Glory, glory hallelujah. Glory, glory hallelujah Glory, glory hallelujah. His soul is marching on.

He's gone to be a soldier in the army of the Lord; (3x) His soul is marching on. (Chorus)

John Brown's knapsack is strapped upon his back. (3x) His soul is marching on.

(Chorus)
His pet lambs will meet him on the way. (3x) His soul is marching on.

(Chorus)
They will hang Jeff Davis to a sour apple tree. (3x) His soul is marching on.

(Chorus)
Now, three rousing cheers for the union. (3x) As we go marching on."

Later that afternoon we headed back to the bucolic little grass airstrip outside Halltown. All of us brought back souvenirs and mementos from Harpers Ferry. I purchased more than enough material – books, maps, and documents concerning John Brown and Harpers Ferry – to enable me to write my award- winning essay. It ended up being sixteen pages long. And, not to my surprise, I found myself stuck in the middle between two opposing forces, my teacher, who was looking for excellence, and my classmates who simply wanted the bell to ring. By far, mine was the best essay turned in that year. But I learned something more than history in writing that essay. I discovered there are some things, some causes that are worth more than my own life. I realized, because of circumstance and conviction, I may someday be faced with a very difficult choice. Would I have the courage to sacrifice my life for a worthy cause? John Brown did. Jesus did. Soldiers in war have done so thousands of times. Indeed, firemen and policemen faced the decision almost daily. I had never really thought about things like that before. I was only seventeen years old; I just wanted to have fun.

The flight back to Roanoke that evening in the waning sunlight was much quieter and more somber than the festive adventure we had experienced that morning. It had been a wonderful trip - one I'll never forget. But somehow the future seemed more uncertain than it did ten hours earlier. Even the appearance of the changeless Blue Ridge Mountains wasn't what it used to be. They looked older and more battle-worn than before. Suddenly, I felt as though they were, in unison, attempting to whisper to me a secret they had dutifully harbored for centuries, but the language was foreign. I felt more closely connected and in tune with them, but at the same time, they offered no clear direction.

Steve and I didn't talk much over the radio, and Larry was more pensive than usual. I suppose each of us had to affirm his own beliefs in his own way. Much like a thought-provoking motion picture, we each had to weigh the discoveries we had unearthed and analyze them emotionally in our hearts and minds.

My thoughts returned again and again to the words Mr. Ewing had spoken that afternoon:

"... It wasn't so much the cause he died for that impresses me — righteous as that cause was. It was the creed of the man himself, the courage to stand up for right — even when no one will stand with you.

"...Frankly, I have to ask myself if I would be able to follow my heart to such lengths. Would I be willing to fight to the death for a cause that I believed was morally right? I don't know. Would I be willing to pick up a gun and fight my fellow countrymen in order to preserve the Constitution of our founding fathers when the current civil law, the legal system tells me that I do not have that right? Could I, with a sound mind and spirit, actually fight against my own police and justice system if I was convinced I was right by the Bible and the Constitution? I just don't know. But, you know, Dave, one day in this very country it may come down to that...."

Gazing down at the pastoral settings of the Shenandoah Valley, I was forced to come to grips with myself concerning the question: Would I ever be able to commit myself as deeply as John Brown did to some cause I thought was worth standing up for? At that moment in time I couldn't answer myself. But I would never be quite the same again. That was the day I experienced my own great awakening.

Chapter Nineteen

The Taste of Humble Pie

"Don't be selfish; don't live to make a good impression on others. Be humble, thinking of others as better than yourself. Don't think only about your own affairs, but be interested in others, too, and what they are doing."

GOD, by way of Paul

Our adventurous trio continued for a few years, eventually adding a fourth member to the group. We befriended Ted Shinault, an expatriated North Carolina farm boy in the spring of 1976. Ted was a different sort of fellow. He was the quintessential honor graduate from the School of Hard Knocks. Born in 1929, while the rumble of the stock market crash was still echoing down Wall Street, Ted faced innumerable hardships as a youngster. His family's small tobacco farm yielded a meager subsistence living at best. Even with her own brood of thirteen children to feed and care for, his mother had no choice but to take in additional laundry to make ends meet. Then, tragically, when Ted was only twelve years old, his father was killed in an accident on the farm. Immediately, things went from bad to insurmountable. Ted was forced to quit school in order to assist his family in simply putting food on the table. It was a hardscrabble life full of toil and sweat; I couldn't have even begun to imagine the deprivation. But, as with so many of the men I've known during my life who grew up during the great depression, Ted was as humble as anyone among them.

I never heard Ted express a personal resentment toward anyone or anything. He was opinionated though. And once he did form an opinion about something an act of Congress wouldn't have budged him an inch. Never one for books and academics, he possessed more common sense than any man I could name. Ted could do anything. He could build anything. They say that when you lose one of your five God-given senses the other four make up the difference. Maybe it was the same with Ted. Maybe his lack of book smarts was negated by his uncanny sense of "extra-physical dynamics."

He learned to fly in 1954. Hardly able to read the Farmers' Almanac, Ted aced the Private Pilot written examination on the first try with a score of 100%. He completely restored a 1936 Ford pickup from scrap parts; he later sold it to a collector from out-of-state. Ted also possessed an admirable sense of character, and he gave up flying in the late 1950s when he and his wife, Ruby, married and started a family. He never felt forced to do so; it was his choice. His beautiful wife and three kids came first. Everything else was elective. There was no money in the bank for flying until later in his life, and that's when I met Ted.

At twenty years of age, I truly believed that I epitomized the archetypical, pansophical young adult American male. I thought I knew everything. I knew exactly what I was going to do with my life. I had set myself on a pathway that would eventually lead to financial success and an enviable level of luxury, beyond which was immorally extravagant. My time was hectically divided between full-time employment at Blue Ridge Steel Co., academic evening classes at Virginia Western Community College, defusing an extremely sexy but emotionally explosive knockout blond, a Rock-'n'-Roll band (I played the saxophone), and building flying time toward a Flight Instructor license. I was busy all day and night, every day and night. But I was slowly inching away from the firm foundation that had upheld my philosophical design since early childhood. My parents could see it; but, I either couldn't, or I didn't want to. I no longer attended my church, the bedrock of my teen years. And my insolence began to affect the relationships I had at the field. The more flying time I logged, the wiser and more confident I became, or so I believed. Foolishly, I began to look down my nose with contempt and mockery at the Old-Timers I had so admired only a few years before. I questioned their experience and wisdom.

"Ah, what do they know anyway?" I'd say to myself. *"They're just getting old. They'd be scared of their own shadows."*

I was young, strong, and full of impatience. I had no more time for gray-haired philosophy.

One pleasant Saturday afternoon at the airport while enjoying a short respite from flying one load of passengers over the city after another, an older man walked alone down the hill toward the office. As I watched him approach the patio I arrogantly speculated to myself that he was probably some "old blue- collar geezer" that wanted to know what it was like to ride in an airplane. I did not stand to greet him. With humility he offered me his hand and introduced himself.

"My name's Ted. Who could I talk to about re-qualifying as a Private Pilot?"

I escorted him inside without saying a word and introduced him to Mr. Hillman. Then I promptly returned to the patio. In just a few minutes the two of them walked back out through the open door to join me. Mr. Hillman asked if I would put Ted in the pilot's seat and take him up for an hour to see if he would be comfortable enough to begin a series of instructional flights that would soon enable him to exercise his pilot privileges once again. I really didn't want to play 'nursemaid', but any flying time was better than no time.

Ted and I took off in Mr. Hillman's blue and white Cessna 172, N2845L, and headed out to the northeast over Botetourt County for *my* hour's worth of free air time. And during that one hour over the beautiful Virginia countryside I began to understand and appreciate a truly extraordinary man. Moreover, during the course of the next sixteen years until his passing, my admiration for his simple honesty and uncanny abilities grew stronger and more indelible. Ted taught me that knowledge cannot be gathered without experience, wisdom cannot be gained without discernment, and that both are gifts from the *One* that mankind has come to know as the 'Son among men'- Jesus, the one who was, is, and always will be, God himself.

In aviation, more so than in almost any other field of endeavor, you must know when to give up and say "That's it; I can't go any further." Sometimes, nature is simply going to win. It's hard for us to admit defeat; it's difficult to say "I was wrong."

One beautiful Sunday morning in June, the four of us: Steve, Larry, Ted, and I met Bob Reed, one of Mr. Hillman's flight instructors, and a student of his before sunrise at the office for a three airplane formation flight over to the Lunenburg County airport in South Central Virginia, about fifty minutes flying time away from Roanoke. The Chamber of Commerce of the city of Victoria was sponsoring a fly-in breakfast and air show that day, and we didn't want to miss it. I'd never been to Lunenburg County before. I considered myself a lay student of history, and there were many Revolutionary and Civil War stories connected to Lunenburg County that had previously caught my attention. Additionally, all of us were more than a little curious about Victoria's secrets concerning its rowdy and lascivious railroad history. We were hoping to catch a ride into town to do some exploring. We had a veritable digest of attractions we wanted to see after our breakfast at the field.

It had taken me a while to warm up to Bob Reed. The first time I met him, when I was fifteen, I saw only an austere military bearing that was resolute and infrangible. Bob was in his early thirties, much younger than the Old-Timers. With his closely cropped hair, and his dark, stern eyes, he was the epitome of a tough-as-nails drill sergeant. Bob had, in fact, spent several years in the Marine Corps. Frankly speaking, I was scared of him, and I avoided him whenever possible. Gradually though, over many months as I listened to him respectfully interact with the older men at the field, I came to regard Bob's unruffled demeanor and wise council, not only about aviation matters, but also the more diurnal events that seem to manipulate our lives, as the erudite wisdom from an older brother or uncle.

———◆◆◆———

The sun still had not broken free from behind Read Mountain, but its beaming entrant rays refracted a spectral showcase off the willowy cirrus clouds high in the eastern sky, and the brilliant multi-colored panorama illuminated an atmosphere of school- boyish anticipation. We had eagerly been looking forward to the trip for three weeks. Hastily reviewing some basic formation flight rules, we loaded up and took off for Lunenburg County airport.

After departing the Woodrum Airport traffic area to the southeast, we formed a loose echelon to the right with Bob leading. The air was smooth, and everything was fine until about fifteen minutes into the flight. While passing near the community of New London, southwest of Lynchburg, we stumbled upon a low-lying blanket of unexpected fog. Like a white eiderdown carpet, it formed a solid underlying shelf to the east that disappeared into the haze. It stretched to the north through the Blue Ridge Mountains, and to the south over the flat Piedmont as far as the eye could see. We discussed the matter over the radio for just a few moments, and then Bob, the only one of us who had earned an instrument rating, announced that he was going to turn around and head back to Roanoke. Steve, piloting the number two ship, replied and wagered that we'd most likely run out of it before long. He voted to continue.

"Come on, guys. Let's go on a little further and see if we can spot where it ends up ahead."

Ted was the pilot-in-command of our airplane. Grasping the seriousness of the low level fog and what its implications could be, he too expressed his desire to turn around while we could still glide to an open pasture in case the engine quit. But I sided with Steve; I thought we should continue. I'd never experienced an engine failure before, and I didn't expect to encounter one then. The modern aircraft engines were immeasurably more reliable than those old rickety tin cans from the "dark ages." And furthermore, in no uncertain terms, I let Ted know exactly how I felt about it.

Without any further delay, Bob banked his Cessna away to the left and called to us on the radio,

"See you, guys. Good luck." That's all he said.

"*That's just great, Bob!*" I flared to myself. Ted then made his decision:

"Dave, it would be foolish for us to continue. I'm turning around."

I didn't want to argue in the airplane, so I didn't say another to word to him. But I was deeply disappointed. I sat and stewed all the way back home. Secretly, I thought Ted was being overly cautious, like a feeble old man. I told Steve we were heading back, and he whined to us.

"Well, dang it all! It ain't no fun just me and Larry goin' alone. I'll see ya'll back at the field."

Within a few minutes we were all safely back on the Hillman ramp. I was no longer in any kind of sociably interacting mood, but I did, albeit reluctantly, agree to go with the group to the Pancake House in Cloverdale for a consolation breakfast. Before we left though, Bob thought to call the Roanoke Flight Service Station on the phone to inquire about the fog bank. He listened attentively before offering a polite "Thank you" to the station employee. After he hung up the phone he looked directly into my eyes and calmly relayed the report in the driest, most professional tone he could possibly muster:

"Flight Service said the fog formed unexpectedly over the entire Mid-Atlantic region at just about sunup. The temperatures across the state dropped lower than they thought they would because of this air mass we got over us right now. He said the last pilot report they got from over that way was from a Twin Bonanza on an IFR flight plan. Lunenburg is socked in tight. The visibility in Richmond is down to one-quarter of a mile. They expect it to lift before ten o'clock."

There was nowhere for me to look except the floor; I couldn't even look at Steve. The silence in Ted's cherry red Ford pickup was searing all the way to Cloverdale. No one said much of anything as we all sat down at our large table in the restaurant. We did have our breakfast that morning at the Pancake House. Bob and his student, and Ted and Larry all enjoyed a hearty country breakfast of pancakes, eggs, biscuits and gravy, grits, and just about everything else you could name. Steve and I both had crow.

Chapter Twenty

To Each His Own Fate

"We value what is beautiful and scorn the useful.
Yet beauty often destroys us.
The stag despised his feet which gave him life.
While valuing the crown which caused him strife."

From, *The Stag and His Reflection Aesop*

Many years ago, when I flew for a commuter airline out of the Raleigh Durham airport in North Carolina, I was the Captain on a flight up to Charleston, West Virginia. At that time we could legally fly under a set of regulations that allowed us to operate under visual flight rules (VFR), as opposed to instrument flight rules (IFR). VFR operation was always my favorite. It allowed me to change altitudes at will, turn in any direction in order to pass over something on the ground I deemed interesting, or to alter my speed as I saw fit. We flew low enough to allow ample sightseeing.

On this beautiful fall afternoon, as we winged across the vast and brilliant West Virginia foliage, I spotted a white pickup truck racing up a gravel road that ascended a high grassy hill topped with a mesa. The road straightened out after it reached the mesa and ran straight-as-an-arrow across to the other side, whereby it came to an abrupt halt. I banked our airplane in order to get a closer look at this innocuous but somehow intriguing sight.

Beyond the end of the road was a sheer cliff that appeared to drop a couple of thousand feet to the bottom of a heavily wooded gully. As I watched the truck speed its way up the hill, immense clouds of dust and dirt being lifted from behind, I wondered to myself if the driver knew what awaited him at the end of the road. If he was not aware of what was up there on the far side of the mesa, then he was obviously headed nowhere fast. From my lofty perch I could see the beginning, at the bottom of the hill, as well as the end, at the top; from his present position he could see neither.

The Bible teaches us that God is like that. The LORD, the creator of all things, can see the beginning and the end at the same time. He is the Alpha and the Omega, and He knows us personally. He will use us for his purposes whether we agree to it or not. If we refuse to acknowledge him he will simply use us for his divine purpose, and then later, after he's finished with us, he'll leave us to our fate. The Bible also teaches that the LORD sends his angels to guard his children, his church. They may use any of His creations to alter the fate of an individual at God's own command.

The arrival of the long winter months after the holidays in Southwestern Virginia seems to usher in a lugubrious atmosphere that settles deeply into the soul with a unique sort of dreariness. Succinct descriptors like bleak, gray, barren, and gloomy seem to match the disconsolateness of mid-winter when the gutter snow is muddied and forsaken Christmas trees lay betrayed and discarded like the empty pizza boxes from yesterdays' party. The mountainous terrain amplifies the dejection by elevating the sepulchral tone into three dimensions. In the spring and summer, the hills proudly unfold their colorful adornment attracting the eye like the Easter display in a Macy's window. But in winter, one would secretly wish the heights to quietly dissolve themselves into the horizon as one would wish for a boorish cousin at a family reunion.

The mountain ridges, along with the valleys they define, create not only their own brumal personalities, but also their own astringent winter weather. As frontal systems move across the Appalachians in winter, they leave behind isolated valley pockets where the air temperatures are free to abandon their customary behavior due solely to the topography. Normally, the air temperature would be expected to decrease as the elevation increases. The higher you climb, the colder the air becomes. This would hold true in most areas of the country. But in the Eastern United States air masses pursue their own apostatic attractions. In winter, cold moist air can settle in the rural valleys while warm fronts arriving from the south and west stealthily drift across the tops of the ridges. The attacking warm air will hold the defending cold air to the surface of the valley floors like an Olympic wrestler pins his opponent. Eventually the cooler air cries "uncle" and gives up its treasured moisture in the form of a cloaking mist – a vain attempt to escape its own weaknesses. This alienation usually occurs under the cover of darkness, as if done so in shame. The byproduct of the estrangement is aptly known as valley fog.

In my late twenties I was offered a job with a small cargo operator in the Richmond, Virginia area flying the daily express mail out of Roanoke Monday through Friday to a rural airport in extreme southwestern Virginia. Without thinking twice, I jumped at the opportunity to build multi-engine flight time, the bane of the non–military-trained commercial pilot. It was the exact type of job I needed to gain the required experience that would enable me to eventually apply for a position with a major airline.

The only reason I was offered the job was because I arrived for my interview in the boss's cluttered hangar office on the appointed day in September dressed just like he was: blue jeans, sweat shirt, baseball cap, and work gloves protruding from my back pocket. I had hitched a ride to Richmond on another freighter, and I thought it only polite that I help the pilot load and unload the aircraft before I walked away. So, as I stood in front of my prospective employer's desk with sweat soaked underarms explaining my rumpled appearance, he stopped me in mid–sentence with the palm of his hand and said, "You're the man for the job. You're now an Airmail Pilot."

Within five days I was checked out in both types of airplanes I would fly on my scheduled mail run, the twin-engine Cessna "Four–Oh–Two," and the Beechcraft Baron. The 402 was larger and could carry more weight. The Baron was sleeker and faster. The volume of mail to be transported on any given day determined which airplane I would use.

The route of my appointed forty-five minute daily commute would most often be flown in VFR conditions at altitudes ranging from five-hundred to ten-thousand feet down the Roanoke River Valley to Blacksburg, across the wide New River Valley to Claytor Lake, then on down the narrower Glade Creek Valley to Wytheville. From there I would follow Interstate Highway 81 through the Great Appalachian Valley until reaching my destination, Abingdon, Virginia – some one-hundred ten nautical miles southwest of Roanoke. After unloading and securing the airplane I would spend the better part of each day in what I came to know as my home away from home.

I made use of my time in Abingdon after I had arrived with the mail from Roanoke. I taught a few flying students at the local FBO (Fixed Base Operation). I enrolled in a couple of classes in a nearby college. And I invested time and energy tracing the lives of several prominent figures in history that influenced the region, like the backwoods explorer Daniel Boone, whom we have to thank for the slang term of the U.S. Dollar: "Buck," short for "buckskins"

Incorporated in the year 1778, "Bingdon," as it was affectionately nicknamed, was a vibrant and artsy little community close to the Virginia – Tennessee border. Located in Washington County, Virginia, Abingdon was the seat of the Federal District Court for the Tri-State area, including Bristol, Kingsport, and Johnson City, Tennessee. Because of this herald, a dichotomy of class structures was very apparent. On the one hand, rural Appalachian life on the farms and in the villages surrounding Abingdon had changed little, except for the conveniences of modern technology, in the last one-hundred years. On the other, the prestige and influence of the blue-blooded "gifted class" who personified the law of the land (legem terrae), gave the bustling principality an aristocratic pride like a diadem on a hilltop.

In due time I came to know each airplane intimately. I became as familiar with the idiosyncrasies of each of them as one would become with a trusted automobile. I tolerated flying the 402. This model, the 'C' offered a few improvements over the earlier models. It had a lengthened nose cone to carry extra weight forward. The wing was longer, which aided the lifting and stabilizing characteristics somewhat, and the landing gear had been strengthened to allow for higher gross takeoff weights. It was a rugged, functional airplane. Even so, the Cessna was not the apple of my airman's eye. I thought it was slightly underpowered for the weight it carried, and it was heavy on the controls. The 402 handled more like my dad's old Ford Country Squire station wagon he bought in 1970. It couldn't begin to match the agility, the power, and the responsiveness of the Beechcraft Baron. The Baron was a sportsman's airplane. Flying a Baron, any model of the Baron, was thrilling, as though you were commanding a true thoroughbred, a Lamborghini Murcielago. The difference was rather like escorting your best friend's homely sister to the dance instead of making your grand entrance with an exotic brunette on your arm. Nonetheless, there was one advantage the 402 had over the Baron; it had a large crew door next to the pilot's seat that swung upward allowing easy entry and exit when the cabin was full of cargo. By the end of one day in particular I would witness just how prophetic that door was.

The date was February third, and it was a non-descript morning. The sun was neither fully awake nor still soundly asleep. Producing no shadows, it was enjoying an idle slumber that seemed to give credence to the hazy undercast beneath it. The air was damp, as if it were about to shed a tear simply because, by sheer luck of the draw, this date had already been condemned by mankind as one to be quickly forgotten. It was warm for so early in February. The temperature was in the upper forties. Again, non-descript; neither winter, nor summer - forgettable.

As I tossed the last mail sack through the rear door into the 402 I eyed the tail carefully. I could estimate how the ship would handle according to how much clearance the tail had from the ground after the loading process was completed. The tail was down quite a bit; the center of gravity was obviously near its aft limits. This day she would be self-conscious about her lateral axis.

After securing the cargo net, I waved goodbye to the mail truck driver, Boyle Eggleston. If there was ever a man befitting of his name it was Boyle. He was short and round with skinny legs and arms. At first glance, without even knowing his name, the mind conjured up a cartoonist's image of Humpty Dumpty. His oval head was completely bald, and you had to look closely to confirm he even had eyebrows. His pearly skin emanated a shining opaqueness that made him appear as though he were sweating. It was difficult to look him in the eye and say his name with a straight face. On one occasion, without thinking, I made the foolish mistake of calling him by the nickname I had given him, "Eggy." The stern look he gave me in return left no doubt as to his toleration of such a scurrilous sobriquet, and I could only imagine what his school days had been like as a boy. I never called him Eggy again, at least to his face.

In order to maintain his Saturday-morning-cartoon physique, Boyle was always munching on something, usually out of a large, colorful bag. On this particular day it happened to be animal crackers. Having to transport the heavy mail sacks from the truck to the plane by myself while Boyle stood like the Nabisco automaton was bad enough, but when he began tossing the treats to the birds he spied in the area – even onto the wing of the plane – I could no longer hold my tongue.

"Boyle! You know, the more you feed those birds the more they'll be hanging around here. And birds and airplanes do not mix very well."

He was nonplused, but his expression never wavered. It was his job to ensure I had loaded the airplane and taken off for Abingdon. And he would stand there all day eating animal crackers until I did.

I entered the cockpit through the crew door and started the engines. As was my usual practice unless it was freezing cold, I left the door open as I taxied the airplane to the runway. The cool air blowing in through the large open hatch quickly dissipated the heat my body had generated while loading over one-thousand pounds of mail in only a very few minutes. It also made me feel more like a fighter pilot with the bubble canopy open as I taxied around the airport wearing my brown leather flight jacket.

After completing all the preflight checks I reached up to close and lock the crew door. At that same instant, I received a surprise visitor. A tiny sparrow flew in under my arm through the open hatch. He fluttered around me for an instant then retreated to the rear of the airplane, whereby he settled onto a mail sack with perspicuous content. His congenial chirping seemed to enliven the tone of the lackluster morning as a skilled soloist energizes the virtuosoship of a mediocre band, and the tenor of my disposition was reflected in kind. I had never before seen a bird fly into the interior of an operating airplane. Smiling, I asked him aloud,

"Well, there, little friend, you want to go to Abingdon?"

He seemed eager to experience the thrill of a new home and new friends. So, not having any more time to waste, I pointed the Cessna down the runway, and we lifted off together into the amorphous winter sky.

The mist hanging over the ridges around Roanoke raised my concerns about the possibility of fog as we climbed out of the valley to the west. The dampness of the air testified that there had been a volatile mixing of air masses sometime during the night; the mist was irrefutable proof; like the proverbial smoking gun. Tri–City airport at Bristol, Tennessee was reporting a low overcast condition with about two miles visibility at that time. Since the Abingdon airport was too small to have any official type of weather observation capabilities, I was not allowed by law to file an IFR flight plan with it as my destination. If the weather appeared to be below VFR minimums around the Abingdon area I was required to file an IFR flight plan to the Tri-City, Tennessee airport. Abingdon was located about twenty nautical miles northeast of Tri-City. I would fly directly over Abingdon on my way to my filed destination. If I could see the Abingdon airport as I flew over it, then I would simply cancel my IFR flight plan with Tri-City Approach Control and land at my desired destination, Abingdon.

Even with a full load of mail on board the 402 climbed with uncharacteristic expedience to the filed IFR altitude of six- thousand feet. The reason for this overt impetuosity was the fact that she was lighter than normal. A few days before this morning, my boss had called from Richmond to chastise me for buying and carrying too much fuel out of Roanoke. The FBO at Abingdon sold its avgas at a price that was several cents per gallon less than the one in Roanoke. So, naturally, he wanted me to depart Roanoke with only the legally required amount of fuel in the tanks. I was to purchase the necessary amount of fuel in Abingdon that would reasonably be expected the following day. It was a sound accounting practice. But aviation, by its physical design, was more respectful of God's natural laws than it was of man's addiction to numbers.

I adjusted the airplane's power and trim controls for an economical cruise speed then switched on the autopilot so I could pour a cup of coffee from my thermos bottle and complete the weight and balance paperwork that I would have to surrender upon arrival in Abingdon. We were still flying beneath an obscure overcast in fairly good VFR conditions. The visibility ahead was about twenty miles in haze with only scattered patches of ground-hugging mist here and there. I was hopeful of being able to spot the Abingdon airport if these conditions held. I turned around in my seat to check on my ticketless rider. He was quietly surveying the landscape below, cocking his head as if to recalculate his little brain for future high altitude flight. He did not appear to be anxious in any way. In fact, he seemed to be enjoying the experience of letting someone else do the flying for once.

"If you think this is something, wait till we land!" I advised him.

Approaching the New River Valley, the atmospherics began to change. I noted the outside air temperature was rising. The temperature was now about the same as it had been on the ground in Roanoke. I was flying into an area with a temperature inversion, a warm air mass. That fact, coupled with the upslope clouds over Jefferson Mountain to the north, indicated a high probability of running into valley fog. My eyes strained ahead to locate the meandering New River. If there was fog in the valley it would be seen first in the humid air over the cold water.

I called the Flight Service Station in Roanoke on the radio to receive any updates on the weather at Tri-City. Their observer was still reporting a low overcast with a visibility now of about one mile. While still cautiously optimistic of a successful approach and landing at Abingdon, I was also aware of an insidious local phenomenon that could rear its ugly head if the wind at the Tri-City airport was blowing lightly from the south.

In 1963, the TVA (Tennessee Valley Authority) completed work on a reservoir that would provide a vast area of northeast Tennessee with drinking water and electric power. Much of this reservoir, Boone Lake, was located less than one mile from the runways at the Tri-City airport. When the wind was out of the south the lake would often produce a dense fog that could quickly reduce the forward visibility down the airport's runways to zero.

I asked the Flight Service Station attendant what the wind was doing at Tri-City. He answered,

"One-nine-zero degrees at ten knots."

I then asked him about the temperature and dew-point spread.

"Temperature, one-zero (10 degrees Celsius). Dew-point, one- zero."

My shoulders involuntarily fell; there was no spread. The outside air temperature at the airport was fifty degrees Fahrenheit, and the air temperature required by the *invisible* moisture to produce *visible* moisture (dew–point), was now also fifty degrees Fahrenheit. As if to add insult to injury, the wind had shifted; it was directly out of the south. Collectively, this information did not bode well. It was time to consider my alternatives.

The very first action any pilot will take when faced with the prospect of being unable to land at his intended destination is to "*white-eye*" his fuel gauges. His mind then begins to run hasty calculations of time verses distance estimates. Two questions plant themselves in the foreground with unimpeachable dominance: "How much time do I have left before I run out of fuel, and where can I go that is within that time frame?" Nothing else in the entire world matters at that point. Heart rates increase and respiration deepens as the brain begins gulping its own fuel.

I turned around in my seat and warily advised my new friend.

"Fifty-fifty. You should have gotten out when you could. If we can't get into Abingdon we may be in a world of hurt."

He chose that moment to utter the first audible sound he had made since we left the ground – one plaintive little peep. Somehow, I think he recognized the portentousness in my voice. He remained motionless.

I shook my head in disgust as I surveyed the valley ahead of me. I should have had more fuel on board. Because of my timorous acquiescence to my boss's demands for more costs consciousness, I had unwisely departed from Woodrum

Field with barely enough gas to fly for an hour and a half. I could make it to Tri-City, shoot a couple of approaches, and then fly around for twenty minutes or so before I would exhaust my last drop of fuel. I would then be in command of a three-ton glider; not an attractive prospect over hilly, wooded terrain.

Just as I had expected, three or four miles east of Fort Chiswell I spotted the nemesis I had feared, the revanchist that was so effective at driving man and his clamorous machines from the air and giving it exclusively back to God's creations: valley fog. It was spread before me like the plague on the Nile. As far as I could see down the Great Appalachian Valley, a white wall-to-wall carpet clutched at the bases of the high ridges. Only the loftiest elevations were left exposed to the attenuated sunlight. I felt an undeniable sinking in my heart, like I had said goodbye to hearth and home and had come face-to-face with the disdainful and the uncaring. The friendly mountains I had come to rely on over the last six months as welcomed landmarks and conciliatory affirmations suddenly seemed cold and reproachful, even vindictive. I knew right then I should have turned around and returned to Roanoke. From that point on I felt like I was falling headfirst into a villainous web of deceit infested with sworn enemies.

Part Two

The very idea of failure at a given task is as abhorrent to the human psyche as starvation is to the human body. From the time we are born we are programmed to win, to succeed at all costs, to never, never quit until we conquer the demons opposing us. There is a mysterious entity within our souls that constantly drives us onward toward our ultimate goals even while staring down the very throat of defeat. On success and failure Theodore Roosevelt was quoted in a speech in the year 1910, in Paris, France:

> "It is not the critic who counts, not the man who points out how the strong man stumbled, or where the doer of deeds could have done better. The credit belongs to the man who is actually in the arena, whose face is marred by dust and sweat and blood, who strives valiantly, who errs and comes short again and again, who knows the great enthusiasms, the great devotions, and spends himself in a worthy cause, who at best knows achievement and who at the worst if he fails at least fails while daring greatly so that his place shall never be with those cold and timid souls who know neither victory nor defeat.

Whether through some misguided sense of loyalty to manhood or my own naivety caused by a lack of experience, I girded my loins in a determination to forge ahead and complete my mission. Perhaps somewhere in the back of my mind I was bolstered by the stirring quote the learned Greek writer Herodotus penned in the year 475 BCE while praising the stamina and persistence of the horsed messengers in the service of King Xerxes during the Persian Wars:

"Neither snow, nor rain, nor heat, nor gloom of night stays these couriers from the swift completion of their appointed rounds."

I was an Airmail pilot; I could get through. I would deliver the charge entrusted to me to those who were awaiting its arrival or I would die trying. I could not accept retreat.

Twenty minutes after first spotting the valley fog I was handed off by the Atlanta Air Route Traffic Control Center to the Tri-City Approach Control. The obscuration below me had not abated. In fact, it had become even thicker and more menacing. The controller vectored me over the Abingdon airport, and of course, I saw only grayish white clouds beneath me as I flew past. I had no other choice but to continue on for an IFR approach at the Tri- City airport. The latest weather report broadcasted a slight increase in the ceiling height and a slight improvement in the visibility, but with Boone Lake deploying its formidable marching sheets of fog across the runway like the Persian Immortals at Thermopoly, the visibility raised and lowered alternately at nature's whim. Upon arrival at the decision height on the Instrument Landing System approach, success or failure would be a toss of the coin.

My first approach did not go well. Because the airplane was so devoid of fuel and the center of gravity so far to the rear, I had trouble staying locked onto the glide slope. The machine wanted to porpoise its way down the vertical path. I crossed the threshold of the runway over one-hundred feet high, still in the clouds, and I never did see the pavement. I had no choice but to execute a missed approach and go around to try again. Climbing out for another approach, I studied the fuel gauges carefully. They were fluctuating between empty and about an eighth of a tank each; I estimated I had enough fuel for two more attempts.

While on what amounted to a wide circle south of the airport, I was in clear air above the ground fog, and I could see the mountains around the entire region standing in the vast wading pool of cloud. I scanned the milky horizon searching for any areas that might be in the open, but because of the haze I could see nothing with any promise.

On my second approach I had a better feel of the airplane, and I was able to follow the glide slope more accurately. We reached the decision height with both the glide slope and the localizer needles centered; however, I saw nothing but an opaque windshield in front of me. I held my rate of descent steady for another one-hundred feet. I had no other choice; I was running out of time. At less than one-hundred feet above the still enshrouded runway the coward in me reared its head. I knew the lifesaving harbor was down there below me somewhere, but I could not bring myself to descend any lower. Visions of a violent end prevented me from further probing. I missed again.

On what I knew was my last circle to the south, I informed the controller that I was precariously low on fuel and I had to land. The fuel gauge needles were barely moving now and every minute that passed was merely one step closer to the end of the 'plank'. The controller asked me if I wanted to declare a fuel emergency. Reluctantly, I answered in the affirmative. He told me he would stay with me and keep me over the runway. All I had to do was control my rate of descent until I touched down. It was no promise of a successful outcome, but it offered the best opportunity of walking away under my own power from a broken airplane. It was my last chance. I would live or die on this next approach. I would hit something on or near the airport. My knees had already begun to shake, and my hands trembled at the possibility of having only minutes to live. I couldn't believe I had been so self-deceived. I thought it incredulous that I could slide so easily down the pathway of destruction without seeing any overt warning signs or hearing any alarm bells.

"How did this happen!?" I screamed at myself, rebuking my own dereliction.

I was in trouble, bad trouble. Fate had caught up with me like the Grim Reaper. Without trumpeting its arrival, it slithered next to me, bringing a repulsive stench that fouled all that was good.

As I prepared myself for the last landing attempt, an unorthodox thought came to my mind. I asked the controller if I could change radio frequencies for just a minute in order to broadcast a call on a common air-to-air frequency. I thought there might be a chance, just a slim chance that someone, some other pilot out there might know of a field close by that was open and free of fog. I made four calls in the blind but received no reply. There was nothing but a cold steely silence. It was then that God moved to rescue me from a fate only He could see.

Controlling the airplane with my left hand, I put the microphone in my lap with my right so I could change the radio frequency back to Tri-City Approach. The instant I reached for the radio knob my little sparrow friend, whom I had forgotten about, appeared suddenly in front of my face for three or four seconds distracting me with his fluttering. His unrelenting boisterousness annunciated a singular urgency, as if he were frantically trying to tell me something vital. And then, with like abruptness he was gone, returned to the rear of the cabin without another sound. But those few seconds were all he needed to carryout God's order. Before I could I reach for the second time to switch radio frequencies a lifeline was thrown to me. From the speaker overhead there came an unexpected transmission:

"Elizabethton traffic, Cessna 43477 is downwind runway six for touch-and-go."

I couldn't believe it! There was an airplane shooting touch-and- go landings at Elizabethton, Tennessee. That airport was barely thirteen miles southeast of where I was at that very moment.

Immediately, I turned right toward the little valley airport; I had no time to waste. I switched my radio dials back to the Tri- City Approach frequency and informed the controller that I was headed for Elizabethton in an emergency condition. He said he would call ahead on the landline and inform the airport manager that I was inbound.

Before, as I scanned the horizon for an area free of fog, I could not see the Elizabethton airport because it lay hidden in a blind valley at the base of the regnant Holston Mountain. But as I approached the ridge from the northwest I could plainly see the runway on an elevated sloping tract of farm land at the foot of the mountain. The field was clear and open, but the encroaching blanket of fog was less than half a mile to the west. If not for the higher elevation of the airport, it, like town below it, would also have been encased in thick cloud. I rounded the tip of the wooded ridge, turned east up the valley, lowered the landing gear, and touched down without delay on the only available runway within seventy miles. Ten minutes later the airport was closed due to fog.

———◆◆◆◆———

It has been said with redundancy that experience makes the best teacher. I know for a fact this statement is true. The renowned British Romantic Poet, John Keats, said of experience:

> *"Nothing ever becomes real till it is experienced. Even a proverb is no proverb to you until your life has illustrated it."*
>
> John Keats, 1795–1821

I learned many things that day in early February. I learned that I would have to take care of my own hide because no one else had as much invested in it as I did. I learned that we walk a fine line between life and death, and the laws of physics had no favorites. I learned that I was not indestructible, and that fate will catch up to all of us – sooner rather than later if we're foolish. Most importantly, I learned that the words in the Bible are true and everlasting. God really does control his own creations by his spirit, and he really is watching over me all the time.

From the outside I opened the rear door on the 402 with care so as not to startle God's diminutive creature - whom I named Seth, *"Appointed"*. He didn't make a sound, and I didn't say a word; we just looked at each other for a few blessed moments until a young man walked up from behind me to ask if I was the emergency aircraft coming over from Tri-City.

"Yeah, that's me. Did you tell 'em I was down?"

"No. They hung up before you landed, but they want you to call 'em as soon as you can."

Seth began chirping and flapping anxiously on his mail sack gaining the young man's attention, but he made no movement toward the open door.

"Well, how about that! Did he just fly in there?"

"No, he's been with me the whole time; I brought him from Roanoke. He flew in through the crew door just before I took off."

"Well, I'll be. I've never seen a dumb bird fly inside an airplane before. I seen 'em smashed on the outside though." He said with a laugh.

Jumping up onto the step of the door he crudely chased Seth out of the cabin.

"Shoo. Go on! Get outta here ya stupid bird!"

Seth gave me one last chirp as he flew out through the door and across the field to the west disappearing into the approaching fog. I had to look away.

"Looks like you just barely made it in here. Look at that fog comin' up the slope." He said as he gestured across the ramp.

"Yeah. I had an angel as a co-pilot."

"I thought God was supposed to be your co-pilot."

I weighed the storied apothegm carefully before I shook my head slowly and replied.

"No. The LORD is – with absolutely no doubt – my Director of Operations."

"Well, that's a new one." He said. "But I guess it's true. You need some gas don't cha?"

Around a lump in my throat I answered,

"Yes, I most certainly do, but I'd better call Tri-City first. Can I use your phone?

"Yeah, it's on the desk right through the door over there." He said as he pointed to the office shack.

Obviously, he noticed the dolor on my face because he then asked,

"Are you okay? You look like you just lost your best friend."

Amazed, I turned to look directly at the young man. Could he somehow have known how prophetic his statement was? I almost began to explain…, but I let it go. Then with a wave of my hand, as if discounting the moment, I replied,

"It'll pass."

Chapter Twenty-One

Passing the Torch, Part Two

A few minutes later there was a familiar light knocking at the door – followed immediately thereafter by the extrinsic aggravation of the flight attendant interphone buzzer. John was ready to return from the cabin. I hung up the phone and pressed the door unlocking switch, and he came in with a big smile and two cups of coffee.

"Veronica said she didn't have any Gingerbread cookies, but I've got something better anyway. I warmed up some of my mom's Baklava. It's really good this time. She didn't overdo it on the garlic."

"Garlic!?" I exclaimed.

"No. I'm kidding you." He laughed. "She put a little more cinnamon in it. It's some of the best she's done in a long time."

Veronica came through the door right behind John with a dinner plate mounded with the freshly baked Greek favorite. The aroma was almost invigorating. She took a seat behind me, and the three of us had barely begun to enjoy our dessert when John pointed at the fuel indicators on the lower ECAM.

"Looks like you've been daydreaming again."

I locked my eyes on the little green boxes and was astonished to see that we now had a five-hundred pound fuel imbalance in the opposite direction. The left main tank contained more fuel than the right one did.

"I didn't think I was gone that long." I chuckled to myself. "Man, you just can't trust anybody these days." I replied.

I reconfigured the fuel pump switches above my head, allowing the fuel to rebalance itself once again, this time in the opposite direction.

"Alright, smarty pants; let's see if you can do better." I said to John in jest.

"I'll nail it before I finish my second piece." He replied as he held up his portion of Baklava.

After a few minutes of light-hearted bantering and razzing each other, and everything else pertaining to the company, John and I glanced down at the same time to check on the progress of the fuel balancing procedure. We were both shocked to see that the situation had actually worsened. We were now faced with a fifteen-hundred pound debit in the right tank. It had been only five hundred pounds just a few minutes before.

"Whoa! What's this?" I snapped.

John made an appropriately similar comment, and then our eyes darted in unison to the overhead fuel pump switches. We checked audibly, together, that the switches had been placed in the proper positions to allow fuel to be cross-fed from the left main tank to both engines simultaneously: The crossfeed valve switch was illuminated with a dim blue light, the center tank had no fuel in it, and both fuel pumps in the right main tank were off.

"This is completely crazy." John uttered as he picked up the clipboard to verify what our total fuel level should be by this point in our flight plan.

I stared at the fuel indicators as I watched the numerals diverge before my eyes.

"They're going the wrong way. I can actually sit here and watch them count themselves into oblivion." I stated with blundering authority.

I rechecked the fuel pump switches.

"That's right, isn't it?" I asked John as I pointed at the overhead panel. "I mean, we got `em set right, don't we? The fuel should be going down on the left side and staying put on the right side. Right?"

John's eyes raced between the fuel pump switches, the ECAM gages, and the flight release on the clipboard.

"Well, we should have about fourteen thousand on right now passing abeam Yakutat." He stated.

We both began to carefully add the totals that were indicated in each fuel tank, even though the balance level was becoming more inequitable by the second. Adding the figures we summed to the amount registered on the "fuel used" indicator, we both felt reasonably assured that the airplane still contained the required amount of fuel on board. But the disparity between the tanks was becoming more calamitous with each passing moment. The ECAM fuel tank depiction now indicated a greater than two thousand pound imbalance.

"If that split hits thirty-three hundred pounds it's gonna start flashing at us." John pronounced with an unmistakable dread in his voice. "I wonder just what that means in this case? Does it mean we could actually flame out an engine if we screw this up?" I could see wheels turning in his mind, and it didn't take a genius to see where they were leading him.

"Okay. Let's stop playin' around with this thing. Check the QRH under fuel anomalies and see if there's anything we can do about it." I commanded. "We may have to try to get a hold of maintenance if we can reach `em from here."

John opened the emergency procedure handbook and ran his finger down the list of categories checking to see if there was a listing for fuel imbalance problems. I made the decision to disconnect the autopilot to see if the left wing would begin to drop on its own accord because of the possible weight incongruity between the left and right wings.

"John, I'm gonna turn off the autopilot to see if I can feel anything."

He thought it was a good idea. "Go ahead and try."

Veronica had been relaxing with her shoes off while seated behind us all this time, oblivious to the toxic atmosphere building in the cockpit, and she finally spoke with such a beloved ignorance that it shredded the gossamer veil between my reality and my fantasy like only a child's innocence can.

"Is there something wrong with this airplane?"

By the chaste breath of a lovely young lady, John and I were both broadsided by a viral entelechy no airline pilot would ever willingly admit he dwells on for more than a fleeting moment: '*We hold in our hands tonight the lives of many trusting, unaware human beings. What if I make a dreadful mistake?*' Just as suddenly, I'm sure of it, we both covertly put the thought out of our minds and sacredly vowed to never speak of it. We returned our consciousnesses to the problem at hand.

John then turned patiently toward Veronica, and with a somewhat practiced, patronizing smile, he wisely suggested that she take the rest of the Baklava and offer it to the first-class passengers. She stood with her hand upon the door and pouted,

"I can take a hint, but let me know as soon as you can if we're going to ditch in the ocean. I want to put a scarf on my head because I just got my hair done. Okay, boys?"

With that, she strutted procaciously out the door. In a feeble attempt to return at least a false sense of bravado to the cockpit, I looked again at John and said,

"You know, there's a lot of wisdom in flying boxes around instead of people."

"Yeah, I know. They never complain." He responded.

John then began reading aloud the only section in the Quick Reference Handbook that was applicable to our situation: a four- step procedure to correct a fuel imbalance condition in flight, a common but innocuous problem. It did nothing more than reinforce the steps we had already taken. It did not address the conundrum we currently faced: apparent unrestrained fuel flow from one wing to the other, irrespective of fuel pump operation. This was a new and perplexing enigma. We needed to retreat for a moment and analyze all our information carefully.

Evidently, we were not losing any fuel. All the numbers added up to the correct total that we were supposed to have at the time. The fuel pump switches were set correctly. The crossfeed valve was open. The fuel should have been balancing itself between the two wings. Nevertheless, at least electronically, it was not. So, one of two things was happening: because of some mechanical affectation, such as an unseated fuel cap o-ring producing a spurious pressure differential between the two wing tanks, the fuel was flowing through the transfer line from the right tank to the left. If that were the case, then both engines were being fed fuel from the right tank.

The other possibility was that the fuel was actually flowing in the desired direction, left to right, and only the electronic indicator in the left tank was malfunctioning. Such a scenario presented a whole new set of problems. I voiced my concern to John.

"You know, if the fuel is, in fact, flowing correctly, from the left main tank to both engines, and only the sensors in the left tank are malfunctioning, then how much fuel do we really have in the left tank?"

John agreed.

"That's what I'm worried about. If we're supposed to have about fourteen thousand pounds on board right now, then we'd expect to have around seven thousand pounds in the left tank. But since we've been cross feeding *from* the left tank, then it's somewhat less than that now. And if we keep going like this we could flame out the left engine because of fuel starvation while the fuel indicator falsely shows ten thousand pounds or more."

John then asked me the most poignant question of the night: "What do you want to do?"

Just as he uttered those words the imbalance level reached thirty-three hundred pounds, and the indicator on the ECAM began flashing from dim green to bright green alternately.

"Well, there it is." John mouthed in disgust. "And it's still flowing, fast!"

Whether or not it was connected in any way to the tension in the cockpit at the time, I could not keep my memory from recalling an intrinsic intolerance my brain harbored for too many numbers and letters. Once a workable level of technical data had been absorbed, my mind seemed to reject (as superfluous information), all additional attempts at entreatment.

"Okay." I finally decided. "Let's turn on all the fuel pumps we've got and close the crossfeed valve. We'll assume that the numbers are incorrect. I think we've really got more fuel now in the right tank. Either that, or they're about even. We cross-fed the other direction earlier, remember? I'm going to disconnect the autopilot and see what we've got."

John reached to illuminate the fasten seat belt signs, and I turned on both fuel pumps in the right main tank then closed the crossfeed valve.

"Do you want me to make an announcement about anything?" He asked.

"Just tell `em it may get, I don't know, bumpy." I said.

After John returned from his public address duties I clicked off the autopilot with the anticipation of having to apply positive pressure to the side stick in the opposite direction of a sudden roll to the left. The airplane didn't move an inch. It was completely stable. Somewhat disappointed, I felt like I'd just shot a sleeping elephant in the fanny with a spit wad. I then removed my hand from the side stick controller to see if the airplane would start to bank slowly. We began a very slight climb, no more than one hundred

The Gift

feet per minute, but, for the time being anyway, there was no tendency to bank in either direction.

"Well, there ain't nothing happening here." I spouted.

"Maybe it has to get up to a certain level of imbalance before the thing starts to roll over." John speculated.

"Ah, man, I don't even want to hear it. There's not a thing we can do about it anyway, except maybe fly faster."

We attempted to contact our company's maintenance controller and dispatcher on the company frequency, as well as ARINC on theirs, but were unable to raise either one; we were too far away from both of their receiving antennas. At that point we had about forty minutes to go before reaching Anchorage.

"You want to tell Center we got a problem?" John asked.

"Before we do that, ask him what the weather is at Cordova. I'm sure it's lousy. But in case we need to get in there, we'll be ready." I instructed.

The Cordova weather was bad - worse than Anchorage. The visibility was down to one quarter of a mile in blowing snow, and the runway was covered with three inches of heavy snow over ice. To make matters worse, the winds were howling out of the north – directly across that runway. It was not a good night to attempt a landing in Cordova, Alaska in a transport aircraft that may become laterally unstable at any moment. We were committed; it was Anchorage or nowhere. We informed the Anchorage Center controller that we would need an immediate approach clearance for a landing as much into the wind as possible when we reached the terminal airspace.

Pooling our collective knowledge, neither John nor I could reasonably conclude that the fuel levels, as they were indicating, were accurate. Neither one of us had ever heard of this type of problem happening before. We had no emergency checklist to combat the specific malfunction, and the airplane showed no tendency to bank to the left. In our minds, we had no choice but to conclude that we were faced with an electronic inconsistency in the fuel sensing equipment somewhere between the ECAM and the left main fuel tank. But even if we were experiencing an egregious fuel imbalance emergency, there wasn't much else we could do except get to our destination as quickly as possible.

We calculated that at the estimated touchdown time, assuming the present rate of *transfer* remained stable, we would land with an electronically indicated imbalance of about six thousand pounds. If the sensors in the left main wing tank were dependable, and what we were looking at was true, we would be landing the airplane with one wing almost three tons heavier than the other. Both of us wondered if it could be done safely on a snow-covered runway, or at all for that matter. When we came within radio range of their transceiver, John called ahead to the Anchorage Station Operations to ask them to have a maintenance technician meet us at the gate upon our arrival. The airplane would spend some time in Anchorage.

We touched down on runway '32' at six minutes past eleven o'clock. The ECAM had continued its annoying flash with an indicated fuel imbalance of five thousand seven-hundred pounds when the main wheels contacted the pavement. Because of that disparity, I flew the approach manually at a higher than normal rate of speed while using the least amount of flaps that we could get away with on a snow contaminated runway. We could not risk utilizing the autopilot to fly the airplane. It would have cowardly disconnected itself and bailed out if it had suddenly discovered that it was no longer able to hold a too-heavy wing stable during a critical phase in the approach. Fortunately, the snowfall had decreased in intensity, and the forward visibility had improved to one- half of a mile. The braking action on the eleven thousand foot runway remained good. But even with that, we were not able to slow enough to allow us to exit the runway until the last turnoff, just before the embankment drops precipitously into the icy waters of Cook Inlet.

We taxied the Airbus to the concourse gate and stopped on the 'J' line marker. After setting the parking brake I shut down both engines. While completing our shutdown checklists, John leaned forward, threw me a look that screamed unequivocal exasperation and said exactly what I expected him to say,

"Boy! Let's don't do that again."

I replied trivially, "Yeah, let's go buy the t-shirt."

Veronica and I stood in the forward galley to thank the customers for their patronage while John went to find the mechanic. She leaned into me and covertly inquired about the problem. I whispered into her ear an amalgamated but invalidated diagnosis.

"Computers."

I smiled and nodded as graciously as I could and thanked everyone for flying our airline.

The last passenger to come forward was a young man, perhaps fifteen or sixteen years of age. His face was beaming with delight. His eyes could not conceal an exuberance for something in particular, and I wondered if he would recognize the tribulation in mine. Under one arm were several books and manuals covering a wide range of aviation related subjects from basic aerodynamics to weather charts. He approached me reverently with an outstretched hand.

"Are you the captain?" He asked with awe in his voice.

I could not constrain the grin on my face. But this cherubic genuflection was not the subject of my untimely amusement. What struck me as being ridiculously extrinsical enough to be hilarious was the idea that this innocent weanling, so gloriously ignorant of how close he had just come to possibly not seeing his next birthday, was still enraptured with the very idea of flying.

"I certainly am." I chuckled. "My name's Dave. What's yours?" "I'm Ted. Ted Colburn. But my friends call me 'T. C.'"

We shook hands, and then he timidly asked if I had time to answer a couple of questions about flying and airline procedures. Honestly, I didn't feel like talking to anyone. My mind was still replaying the harried events from the last hour, and I had a hundred things to do: I needed to document insipient mechanical problems, fill out event reports, talk to the mechanics and the maintenance controller, coordinate the transportation to the hotel; I was tired and frustrated. My excuse to say no was on the very tip of my tongue when I had a sudden change of heart. I looked again into his eyes, and instantly, a quiet voice within me said "Do it."

"Sure. Come on in and have a seat. Don't know if I can answer all your questions, but I'll do my best."

We sat and talked together in the cockpit for a few minutes while I demonstrated some basic procedures that we used, and I answered some specific questions he'd been waiting to ask. Gradually, I began to recognize a familiar, puerile character trait. The young man carried an unmistakable passion in his soul for aviation. The very same passion had all but consumed me many years earlier, but had been lost in the antipathetic world of air commerce. He told me he had already soloed a Cessna 152, and he was studying for his Private Pilot's license. He described in vivid detail the small county airport in Kentucky where he spent most of his time after school and on weekends. He said he earned his flying time by working for his instructor – washing airplanes and doing odd jobs around the field.

I was imparadised by his fervent testimonies. His gallery of tales was infinitely more interesting than anything I could have told him about my job. Listening to Ted adulate life at his little airport, and the pleasant weekends spent there, rekindled my own ardency for the very same joys – enchantments that I had all but forgotten. How wonderful those simple pleasures were.

I had become entangled with a technological, money-hungry behemoth. What was worse, I had adopted its self-imposed, monocratic philosophy as my own acclaimed dogma. I was a "Major Airline Captain." I ran with the big dogs. In my own mind I represented something that was bigger and better than anyone else. In a shocking revelation I realized I no longer carried with me the simplistic truths and beliefs I had accepted as my calling long ago. As I felt the impenetrable wall around me begin to crumble, my mind's eye began to soften and focus on the old-timers and Hillman Flying Service, on the old DC-3s, and Uncle Bernard in his Ag Cat, and the little red brick church with the tall white steeple beneath the giant poplar trees where I spent my guarded youth….

The brief time Ted and I shared together flew by much too quickly, but we both had responsibilities to tend to. I bid him farewell and best wishes for his future. He thanked me profusely for my time and advice. I watched him collect his things and then disappear around the corner. It was time to return to reality.

Reaching for the Flight Operations Manual in my flight bag, my fingers involuntarily enclosed themselves around a small but very familiar object. Instantly, I knew exactly what I needed to do at that moment. I raced up the jet bridge through the concourse door and spotted Ted walking briskly toward the terminal. He turned as I called out after him. His perplexity was quickly displaced by verve. I ushered him off to the side of the aisle way and explained that I had forgotten to give him something.

"Ted, I want to give you this gift, because I know that someday you're going to fly for a major airline. I can't recommend it because, I also know that it may rob you of the passion in your heart you have for aviation. But, I know you're going to make flying your profession.

"Now, there are two items in this box; one is more important in what it represents than the other one is. But they are linked inexorably together for a reason; not just to form the gift in this box, but for a much deeper meaning than that. There is a duality in their purpose together. Each of the two elements of this gift represent something very important that you will need to find in your own life. I want you to take this gift and keep it until you discover the meaning behind each element and what they represent together. It may take years for you to discover these things, or it could happen tomorrow. But I want you to promise me that after you do find it you will someday pass this gift on to another youngster. You'll know when that time comes, and you'll know who that young person is. Do you promise me that you'll do this?"

Ted was puzzled, as I remembered I had been, but there wasn't much else he could say except,

"Yes, I promise."

I then reached into my pocket and retrieved a tattered and faded jewelry box. As I opened it and removed a plain gold cross attached to a simple gold chain and held it in front of him, I said these words:

"A very wise man gave me this a long time ago and made me promise him the same thing you just promised me. Now I'm giving it to you. I know this all sounds really strange, but just a few minutes ago I realized that I discovered its meaning a long time ago in a cotton field in Mississippi."

Appendix

1. Aileron   Hinged control surface on the trailing edge of an airplane wingtip

2. Center   Atlanta Air Route Traffic Control Center. One in a network of radar complexes around the country having jurisdiction over cross-country IFR aircraft.

3. DC-3   Douglas Commercial Corporation Model number 3

4. DC-9   Douglas Commercial Corporation Model number 9

5. DME   Distance Measuring Equipment

6. ECAM   Electronic Centralized Aircraft Monitoring display unit. Consists of two display units in the forward, center instrument panel.

7. FBO   Fixed Base Operation. A non-airline business servicing General Aviation (Private) aircraft and pilots.

8. FLAP   Large movable surface on the inboard trailing edge of an aircraft wing.

9. Flight Service   Federally operated civil aviation pilot weather and flight operations station.

10. Glide Slope   Electronic vertical guidance.

11. J523   "J" High altitude jet routes.

12. Lateral Axis   Imaginary line stretching from wingtip to wingtip. Pitch is affected around the lateral axis.

13. Localizer   Electronic horizontal guidance

14. NASA   National Aeronautics and Space Administration

15. Nautical   A Nautical mile equals 6,072 feet, or 1.15 Statute miles

16. QRH   Quick Reference Handbook (nonstandard checklist)

17. RADAR   Radio Detection and Ranging

18. RMI   Radio Magnetic Indicator

19. Statute   Statue mile equals 5,280 feet.

20. VOR   Very-High-Frequency Omni-Directional Radio navigation range

21. Vref   "V" equals velocity. "ref" equals reference speed.

22. Wind Sock   A simple cloth wind direction and velocity indicator.

Acknowledgments

This is a work of inspiration, due solely to the LORD's gift of salvation, given to all who are called to be his children, his sheep. We hear his voice and recognize it. If we're wise we follow it. Therefore, I wish to acknowledge the LORD as the real author of this work. I simply used the 'pictures' in my memory as a guide to what I felt he wanted me to say in his behalf.

I also want to say thank you to the many wise men that have influenced me and kept me within the boundaries of Christian morality until I dedicated my life to doing the LORD's work. Thanks to my dad, Clyde W. Sandidge, Mr. Wesley V. Hillman, Mr. Ted Shinault, Pastor Mark Martin, Pastor Brad Eberly and my grandfather, Elmo Otho Ward. Witnessing honor such as these men possess is truly a gift in itself.

Special thanks goes to the Trenbeath family: Jim, Dorothy, Rachel, and David, for their patience in attempting to fit a fine literary saddle on an ox.

Dave Sandidge

Bibliography

Bogle, John, *Enough: True Measures of Money, Business, and life.* Hoboken, New Jersey, John Wiley & Sons, 2009

Bowden, Henry, W., *Puritanism, Puritans,* (Online) available http://www.mb-soft.com/believe/txc/puritani.htm August 7, 2008

Brown, John, *Brown on Brown*, Personal letter to Mr. Henry Stearns (Online) available http://www.law.umkc.edu/faculty/projects/ftrials/johnbrown/ browntohenrystearns.html August 5, 2008

Casselman, Bill, *Snow Motto Has Ancient Source*, (Online) available http://www.billcasselman.com August 15, 2009

DuBOIS, W.E.B., *John Brown, A Biography*, Armonk, N.Y., London, England, 1909

Edwards, Jonathan, Jr. D.D., *The Necessity of Atonement, Sermon I,* (Online) available http://gospeltruth.net/Edwards atonement/edwards01 August 13, 2008

Ewing, Daniel, R., Personal interview, October 20, 1973

Faust, Patricia, L., *John Brown*, Historical Times Encyclopedia of the Civil War, (Online) available http://www.civilwarhome.com/johnbrownbio.htm

Gann, Ernest, K. *Fate Is the Hunter, New York, N.Y., Simon & Schuster, 1961*

Guillemette, Roger, *U.S. Centennial of Flight Commission*, Crop Dusters, (Online) available http://www.centennialofflight.gov/essay/General_Aviation/ dusting/ GA16.htm July 26, 2008

Harper, Timothy, *Crop Dusters,* The Beginning of an Airline, (Online) available http://www.rootsweb.ancestry.com July 26, 2008 Hillman, Wesley, V. Personal interview, June 8, 2008

Hilltop House, *Historic Hilltop House, Hotel and Restaurant,* (Online) available http://hilltophousehotel.com/ AboutHilltop.htm August 20, 2008

I.P.M.S. *Roscoe Turner Web Page*, (Online) available http://www.ipmsroscoeturner.org/rtmain.html July 29, 2008

Jefferson, Thomas. "*Harpers Ferry National Historical Park*" (Online) available http://www.nps.gov/archive/hafe/ jeffrock.htm August 5, 2008

Jessen, Gene Nora, *The Ninety-Nines, The 1929 Air Race,* "99 News Magazine" (Online) available http://www.ninety-nines.org/1929airrace.html July 25, 2008

Minkema, Kenneth, P. "*Jonathan Edwards's Defense of Slavery*" (Online) available http://historycooperative.org/ journals/ mhr/4/minkema.html, August 19, 2008

Personalities, *The lovable and flamboyant aviator*, (Online) available http://www.fiddlersgreen.net/AC/personalities August 23, 2008

Resource Bank, *Judgment Day, Africans in America,* (Online) available http://www.pbs.org/wgbh/aia/part4/4p1550.html September 3, 2008

Reynolds, David, S. "*The Party, John Brown, Abolitionist: The Man Who Killed Slavery, Sparked the Civil War, and Seeded Civil Rights.*" (Online) available http://www.kansashistory. us/johnbrown.html

Thaden, Louise, *High, Wide, and Frightened* The University of Arkansas Press, 2004

Virginia, *100 Mountains of Prominence*, U.S. Geological Survey, (Online) available http://www.peaklist.org/Uslists/ VA1000.html July 7, 2008

Virginia is for Lovers, *Shenandoah National Park*, (Online) available http://www.virginia.org/site/features. asp?featureid-356 August 9, 2008

West Virginia Web, *Harpers Ferry, Jefferson County, West Virginia* (Online) available http://wvweb.com/cities/ harpers ferry, August 8, 2008.

Wikipedia, *Harpers Ferry, West Virginia,* (Online) available http://en.wikipedia.org/wiki/Harpers_Ferry, August 10, 2008

Zinn, Howard, *A People's History of the United States, 1492 – Present,* New York, N.Y.: HarperCollins, 1999

59430328R00168

Made in the USA
Middletown, DE
21 December 2017